WARTIME RAPE AND SEXUAL VIOLENCE

WARTIME RAPE AND SEXUAL VIOLENCE

An examination of the perpetrators, motivations, and functions of sexual violence against jewish women during the holocaust

Alana Fangrad

Graduate Program in History

A cognate essay submitted in partial fulfillment of
the requirements for the degree of Masters of Arts in History

The School of Graduate and Postdoctoral Studies

The University of Western Ontario

London, Ontario, Canada

authorHOUSE®

AuthorHouse™ LLC
1663 Liberty Drive
Bloomington, IN 47403
www.authorhouse.com
Phone: 1-800-839-8640

Published by AuthorHouse 10/19/2013

ISBN: 978-1-4918-2269-2 (sc)
ISBN: 978-1-4918-2267-8 (hc)
ISBN: 978-1-4918-2268-5 (e)

Library of Congress Control Number: 2013918012

TABLE OF CONTENTS

ACKNOWLEDGEMENTS

Upon the completion of this cognate, there are a number of people I wish to extend my gratitude to:

At Western University, my first thanks go to Karen Priestman, my supervisor, without whom this work would have been, on so many levels, impossible. I have benefited immensely from your understanding, experience, dedication and wisdom throughout this process, which started only with a vague idea. Thank you for your inspiration and support. Your constructive and thought-provoking comments and advice have been essential in writing this cognate. Thank you!

I am also grateful to the faculty and staff in the history department at Western. Special thanks to Dr. Katherine McKenna whose insightful teachings have helped me widen my perspective of histories of women.

I would also like to thank my support system-my best friends: Liz, Meaghan, and Taryn, thank you for always listening, and motivating me to reach my potential in every dimension of my life. I am so grateful for our friendship.

Adam, thank you for teaching me to trust in my abilities, and for your unconditional love and support throughout my academic journey. Your kindness knows no bounds and for that I love you.

Finally, I would like to thank the individuals most important to me—my family. My sisters, Megan and Rachel, thank you for all the distractions, for all the fun and happiness! You are a constant reminder of the beauty in the present and the exciting prospects in the future. Gramma and Poppa, thank you for all the love and prayers. Grandpa, thank you introducing me the study of history. It is through your teaching, knowledge, and wisdom that history became my passion. Mom and Dad thank you for your genuine interest in my studies, and your continuous encouragement, love and unfaltering support. I am forever grateful.

SECTION I

INTRODUCTION

Across Europe—in ghettos, camps, and brothels—Jewish women were sexually violated by German men—members of the Einsatzgruppen, the Wehrmacht, and even the SS. While this revelation may seem obvious—rape and sexual violence has long been a byproduct of war—in fact, this is a topic which has been largely ignored by Holocaust scholars until recently. This is for several reasons. First, gender and women's history was not seriously applied to the Holocaust until the 1980's. Even then, scholars questioned whether a focus strictly on women would imply a hierarchy of suffering and trivialize the suffering of all Jewish victims.[1] Second, Holocaust historians were generally

---

[1] In particular, Jewish Historian Cynthia Ozick argues that a focus on women would trivialize the suffering of all Jewish victims and the Holocaust, "happened to all Jews who were not seen as men, women or children but as Jews." See, Elizabeth Baer and Myrna Goldenberg, "Introduction," in *Experience and Expression: Women, The Nazis, and the Holocaust,* ed., Elizabeth Baer and Myrna Goldenberg (Detroit: Wayne State University Press, 2003), xviii.

1

uncomfortable with the subject of sexual violence and the topic
was considered taboo. Third, this taboo was further reinforced
by the reluctance of survivors to discuss sexual violence in their
memoirs and testimonies, with many female survivors minimizing
the significance of the specifically sexual aspects of their Holocaust
experience.[2] Fourth, a pervasive assumption that *Rassenschande*
or race defilement laws largely deterred Nazis from committing
acts of sexual violence against women prevented scholars
from pursuing the topic.[3] This assumption was based on the
absence of *Rassenschande* cases involving German Wehrmacht,
Einsatzgruppen, and SS men and Jewish women. This assumption
has only recently begun to be challenged by historians who insist
that oral testimonies and memoirs constitute a legitimate source

---

[2]   For example, as a child, Jewish female survivor 'Pauline' experienced
       repeated sexual molestation in hiding. She minimizes her experience
       asserting, "in respect of what happened, seeing our relatives dying and
       taken away, then seeing the ghetto . . . burn and seeing people jumping
       out and burned. Is this molestation important?" See Joan Ringelheim,
       "The Split Between Gender and the Holocaust," in *Women in the
       Holocaust,* ed., Dalia Ofer and Lenore J. Weitzman (London: Yale
       University Press, 1998), 343 (Citing unnamed survivor's testimony)
[3]   Some historians have used the laws against *Rassenschande* to conclude
       that Germans would not rape Jewish women. In particular, Dalia Ofer
       and Lenore J. Weitzman argue that because of German racial policy
       incidences of rape were rare, in, *Women in the Holocaust,* 7-8; Jack
       M. Morrison claims that Rassenchande laws were "overwhelmingly
       obeyed" in, *Ravensbruck: Everyday life in a Women's Concentration
       Camp, 1939-45* (Princeton, 2000), 177-178. Vera Laska argues that the
       rape of Jewish women was rare, relying on the assumption that Germans
       who violated Nazi racial laws were harshly punished, in, "Women and
       the Holocaust: The Case of German and German Jewish Women," in
       Different Voices: Women and the Holocaust, ed., Carol Rittner and John
       K. Roth (New York: Paragon House, 1993), 265.

base and provide evidence that Jewish women were indeed victims of sexual violence.[4] Using such memoirs and oral testimonies of Jewish survivors, this study will build upon this emerging body of literature to show that Jewish women indeed endured sexual violence at the hands of the Germans and that this practice was so widespread that it became an integral element of the process of annihilation carried out by the Nazis.

---

[4]   See, Jonathon Friedman, *Speaking the Unspeakable: Essays on Sexuality, Gender, and Holocaust* (University Press of America, 2002), 5-6; Friedman argues that there is a substantial body of testimonies and memoirs by both victims and witnesses that serve as evidence that Jewish women were exploited sexually during the Holocaust. As long as these sources are critically evaluated and held to the same empirical standards as all other historical sources, their legitimacy, he asserts, should not be overlooked or discredited.
See, also, Zoe Waxman, *Writing the Holocaust: Identity, Testimony, Representation (*Oxford: Oxford University Press, 2006), 5, 186-188; Waxman insists that oral testimonies and memoirs are a vital source of evidence, for without them, the Holocaust would remain a period of history never fully explore or comprehended. Moreover, testimonies can reveal 'difficult' experiences outside the dictates of traditional female narratives, such as sexual violence.
See, especially, Caroline Schaumann "The Reliability of Survivor Narratives of the Holocaust" in *History in Dispute, Vol. 11: The Holocaust, 1933-1945.* ed., Benjamin Frankel (St. James Press, 1999). Schaumann argues that survivor narratives are a rich and valuable source of evidence that provides both eyewitness testimony and a measure of the emotional effect of the Holocaust. Moreover, Schaumann contends that survivor testimonies can more adequately convey a sense of the magnitude of horrors that official documentation cannot.

Historiography

As a result of groundbreaking studies that have appeared between the second half of the 1980's and the beginning of the twenty-first century, the study of women in the Holocaust has become both a subject of undeniable importance and the driving force behind the establishment of histories of German sexuality within the wider field of Holocaust studies. For many reasons, before the 1970's, the subject of women and the Holocaust received little attention from scholars. First, from the immediate postwar years until the 1960's and 1970's, the field of Holocaust studies itself was still developing and limited in scope. Only as historians broadened their areas of research did questions about women begin to be considered.[5] Second, it was not until the 1970's era of 'second-wave feminism' that a growing awareness of women's history and its importance emerged. New academic trends and developments in women's studies, characterized by a strong emphasis on gender-related experiences, heightened interest and raised issues about women in the wider field of Holocaust studies. As a result of feminist scholarship, a growing interest in using women's perspectives to comprehend the Holocaust emerged, and the concept of gender as an analytical tool developed.[6] Third, the state of source material was limited. Historian Judith Baumel notes that it was not until the late 1970's that a majority of Jewish source material became available, and survivor memoirs as well as oral testimonies began to appear in quantities sufficient to advance the

---

[5]   See Judith Tydor Baumel, *Double Jeopardy: Gender and the Holocaust* (London: Vallentine Mitchell, 1998), 46-52.

[6]   Ibid.

area of research.[7] Thus, the study of women and the Holocaust emerged as a result of developments in the wider field of Holocaust studies, the growth of women's studies as a historical field, and the proliferation of available sources.

Systematic analytical research on the subject of gender and its integration into Holocaust studies began in the early 1980's. These early studies aimed to render women visible within Holocaust history by adding to the general knowledge about women's experiences in both the Holocaust and Nazi period, and challenged the traditional canon of Holocaust literature that was so clearly male-dominated.[8] As Jewish historian Paula Hyman points out, most Holocaust scholars had presumed the experiences of men and women to be identical, and "spoke explicitly of men but implied that women were included in the category of man," marginalizing women as appendages to male actors.[9] Early feminist scholars such as Joan Ringelheim, Myrna Goldenberg, Ellen Fine, Sybil Milton, and Marlene Heinemann focused their research on women's resourcefulness, their daily lives, their particular strengths and

---

[7]   Ibid, 50.

[8]   Joan Ringelheim and Esther Katz, ed., *Proceedings of the Conference on Women Surviving the Holocaust* (New York: Institute for Research in History, 1983), 1.

[9]   Paula Hyman, "Gender and Jewish History," *Tikkun* 3:1 (1988): 35.

vulnerabilities, and male and female differences, while the topic of sexual violence remained virtually non-existent. [10]

Much of this early research sparked controversy over the legitimacy of a gendered study of the Holocaust. Survivors, alongside small groups of feminist and Jewish historians questioned a gendered approach, fearful that it would create

---

[10] Ringelheim's work compared the vulnerabilities of men and women under the Nazis wherein she concluded that, "Jewish women suffered both as Jews and as women from antisemitism and sexism in their genocidal forms," thereby determining that women were more vulnerable than men because of their sex, in *Proceedings of the Conference on Women Surviving the Holocaust,* 1-8.
Goldenberg examines women's unique strengths in concentration camps and focuses on their resourcefulness in "Lessons Learned from Gentle Heroism: Women's Holocaust Narratives," *The Annals of the American Academy of Political and Social Science* (January 1996): 78-93.
Ellen Fine's work isolates gender-based Holocaust experiences and examines vulnerabilities unique to women in, "Women Writers and the Holocaust: Strategies for Survival," in *Reflections of the Holocaust in Art and Literature,* ed. Randolph Braham (New York: Columbia University Press, 1990), 79-95.
Milton researches survival patterns inside camps and suggests women were more resourceful than men in "Women and the Holocaust: The Case of German and German-Jewish Women," in *When Biology became Destiny: Women in Weimar and Nazi Germany,* ed. Renate Bridenthal, Atina Grossman, and Marion Kaplan (New York: Monthly Review Press, 1984), 297-333. For Milton's more recent work on the subject see also, "Women's Survival Skills" in *The Holocaust,* ed. Donald L. Niewyk (Boston: Wadsworth Cengage Learning, 2011), 120-122.
Marlene Heinemann analyzes the difference between men and women through the comparison of female and male testimonies and examines female specific experiences such as sterilization, pregnancy and sexual victimization in, *Gender and Destiny: Women Writers and the Holocaust* (New York: Greenwood Press, 1986).

hierarchies of suffering, and invite unethical comparisons and judgments between male and female victims.[11] Many also believed this kind of research would lead to misguided research questions that would trivialize the suffering of all Jews. Did men or women cope better with their circumstances? Who was stronger? Who suffered more? There was also a strong reluctance amongst female survivors to discuss issues that could invite moral judgment, such as cruelty among women in the camps, sex for barter, and female homosexuality.[12] Reluctance to address issues outside traditional female Holocaust narratives continued to persist into more recent years, as did challenges to the legitimacy of gendered approaches, factors that indubitably contributed to relegating the subject of sexual violence to the margins of Holocaust history.

In the 1990's, Soviet archives were opened to Western historians as a result of the fall of Communism. These newly available sources had a profound effect on Holocaust studies, expanding and diversifying the field dramatically. It was in this atmosphere that new historical interpretations of women's experiences emerged, and the subject of sexual violence began to

---

[11] Elizabeth Baer and Myrna Goldenberg, "Introduction," in *"Experience and Expression: Women, The Nazis, and the Holocaust,* ed., Elizabeth Baer and Myrna Goldenberg (Detroit: Wayne State University Press, 2003), xviii. See especially, Jewish Historian, Cynthia Ozick, in *Women in the Holocaust,* ed. Ofer and Weitzman, 348-349; More recent criticisms are made by, Pascale Bos wherein she acknowledges the importance of gendered approaches, however criticizes early feminist research focuses, and their emphasis on Nazi sexism which she argues seems exaggerated and misplaced in "Women and the Holocaust: Analyzing Gender Difference."

[12] See, Joan Ringelheim, "The Split Between Gender and the Holocaust," in *Women and the Holocaust,* ed. Ofer and Weitzman, 348-349.

be raised.[13] One of the most influential books of the early 1990's was Carol Rittner and John Roth's anthology, *Different Voices: Women and the Holocaust.14* It made a significant contribution to the field, meeting the needs for topical diversification, emphasizing not only the public aspects of women's experience but also the personal ones, such as invasive gynecological examinations, pregnancy, infanticide, and abortion.[15] Another significant publication of the decade was Dalia Ofer and Lenore Weitzman's anthology, *Women in the Holocaust,* which included essays that touched on aspects of sexual violence, including a critical analysis of the treatment and fate of pregnant Jewish women during the

---

[13]   M. Goldenberg, "Different Horrors, Same Hell: Women Remembering the Holocaust," in *Thinking the Unthinkable,* ed., Roger Gottlieb (New York: Paulist Press, 1990), 150-166; Carol Rittner and John Roth, ed. *Different Voices: Women and the Holocaust,* (New York: Paragon House, 1993); Dalia Ofer and Lenore Weitzman, ed. *Women in the Holocaust,* (New Haven and London, 1998); Judith Baumel, *Double Jeopardy. Gender and the Holocaust,* (London, 1998); Esther Fuchs, ed., *Women and the Holocaust: Narrative and Representation.* (New York: University Press of America, 1999); Lillian Kremer, *Women's Holocaust Writing: Memory and Imagination* (Lincoln and London: University of Nebraska, 1999).

[14]   Carol Rittner and John Roth, ed. *Different Voices: Women and the Holocaust.*

[15]   See especially, Gisela Perl, "A Doctor in Auschwitz," 104-118; and Gisela Bock "Racism and Sexism in Nazi Germany," 161-186, in *Different Voices: Women and the Holocaust.*

Holocaust.[16] According to historians Myrna Goldenberg and Sara
Horowitz, in the concentration camps, visibly pregnant women
were selected for immediate killing, emphasizing the crucial ways
in which female physiology played a significant role in women's
camp experiences.[17] In addition, Goldenberg's study unearths
the subject of sexual violence and argues that studying Jewish
women's experiences separate from that of men was crucial
because women were subjected to both sexual assault and rape.[18]

---

[16] Dalia Ofer and Lenore J. Weitzman ed., *Women in the Holocaust.* Ofer
and Weitzman use gender as their framework for analysis, departing
from previous scholarship in the field by identifying structural sources
of gender differences, which elevates the importance and complexity
of gender, going beyond obvious observations. See, especially, "The
Role of Gender in the Holocaust," in *Women in the Holocaust.* 1-18.
Weitzman and Ofer define four structural sources of gender differences
during the Holocaust: prewar gender roles and responsibilities; Jewish
anticipatory reactions; German policy and treatment of men and women;
and the responses of Jewish men and women to their experiences.

[17] See Myrna Goldenberg, "Memoirs of Auschwitz Survivors: The Burden
of Gender," 329; Sara Horowitz, "Women in Holocaust Literature:
Engendering Trauma Memory," 365-366; in *Women in the Holocaust,*
ed. Ofer and Weitzman.

[18] See, Myrna Goldenberg, "From a World Beyond: Women and the
Holocaust," *Feminist Studies* 22 (1996), 667-87. Goldenberg's assertion,
although critical for acknowledging the existence of sexual violence,
fails to adequately acknowledge that the threat of sexual violence was
universal and constituted a major cause of trauma, and even death
for both men and women. The claim that only women dealt with the
threat of sexual violence is somewhat superficial, as recent studies
have demonstrated that men were also victims of sexual violence, and
perpetrators of sexual violence were not solely motivated by a desire
for sex, as sexual violence is both an expression of masculinity and
racial superiority. See especially, Annette Timm, "Sex with a Purpose"
in *Sexuality and German Fascism,* ed., Dagmar Herzog (New York and
Oxford: Berghan Books, 2002).

Building upon the key body of work produced in the 1990's, studies of women and the Holocaust appearing in the twenty-first century encouraged topical diversification, while the challenges to the legitimacy of gendered analysis gradually diminished.[19] Scholars became increasingly analytical, balanced and critical, moving away from overgeneralized and superficial assertions, and recognizing the need to redress the pitfalls of earlier scholarship.[20] Most important to the development of the field was the emergence of studies that approached the study of women and the Holocaust with a more methodical and inclusive approach. Recent studies have increasingly acknowledged the importance of both the "human" experience shared by Jewish men and women alike, and experiences that possessed clear gender characteristics, deriving

---

[19]   It is important to note, however, that critics and skeptics do remain. For example, see, Lawrence Langer, *Preempting the Holocaust* (Yale University Press, 2000), 43-48. Langer rejects gendered approaches, arguing that gender differences were insignificant in the larger context of mass suffering and death.

[20]   Early scholarship tended to research women's history with a set agenda, and there was a tendency to glorify women's behaviour. Zoe Waxman argues that these studies portrayed female survivors as unproblematic victims in the attempt to promote images of human dignity. See, Zoe Waxman, *Writing the Holocaust: Identity, Testimony, Representation* (Oxford: Oxford University Press, 2006), 125-129.

Much of the research also focused too heavily on pregnancy, menstruation, forced-sterilization, and abortion, presenting the experiences of women exclusively in terms of sexuality. Elizabeth Heinemann contends that these studies fail to acknowledge that women's sexuality did not create uniquely female experiences because sexuality was uniquely female, but rather, because men's sexuality shaped different experiences. See, "Sexuality and Nazism: The Doubly Unspeakable," in *Sexuality and German Fascism,* 23-65.

from both physiology, and Nazi ideology.[21] Also significant was the integration of histories of German sexuality, Nazi racial ideology, and wartime rape into the sphere of study.[22]

Until the pioneering work of Elizabeth Heinemann, Annette Timm, and Dagmar Herzog,[23] scholars had long emphasized the sexual repressiveness of the National Socialist regime, maintaining that sex was regarded as serving a purely functional purpose, and was not for pleasure.[24] The work of Dagmar Herzog, in particular, has proven otherwise, highlighting the ways in which the Nazis were in fact preoccupied with sexuality, and its regulation. The

---

[21]   See, especially, Na'ama Shik, "Infinite Loneliness: Some aspects of the Lives of Jewish Women in the Auschwitz Camps According to Testimonies and Autobiographies Written Between 1945 and 1948" in *Lessons and Legacies VIII: From Generation to Generation.* ed., Peter Hayes and Doris L. Bergen (Northwestern University Press, 2008).

[22]   For in depth analysis on the theory of rape during wartime, see Susan Brownmiller, *Against Our Will: Men, Women and Rape* (New York: Simon and Schuster, 1975). Brownmiller argues that rape is the quintessential act in which a perpetrator demonstrates to his victim that they are conquered by his superiority, strength and power. Rape was thus a perfectly logical form of violence within the framework of Nazism, as the Nazis strove to prove themselves the master race.

[23]   See, Annette Timm, "Sex with a Purpose: Prostitution, Venereal Disease, and Militarized Masculinity in the Third Reich," 223-255; Elizabeth Heinemann, "Sexuality and Nazism: The Doubly Unspeakable?" 31-65 in *Sexuality and German Fascism*, ed., Dagmar Herzog. See also, Dagmar Herzog, ed. *Sex After Fascism: Memory and Morality in Twentieth Century Germany,* (Princeton: Princeton University Press, 2005).

[24]   For example, historian of German history, George Mosse argues that the Nazis were both sexually repressed and sex hostile, in, *Nationalism and Sexuality: Respectability and Abnormal Sexuality in Modern Europe,* (New York: Howard Fertig, 1985).

Nazi regime not only promoted extra-marital sex, but also used sex as a reward for both officers and prisoners who went to brothels established by the regime.[25] Furthermore, the integral importance of sex to the German perpetrators, Herzog highlights, motivated them to break the rules, and while German leadership was aware of the gross sexual abuses perpetrated by its own men, they did little to prevent these crimes from occurring. Indeed, Monika Flaschka's work on the intersection of rape, race and gender, reinforces this point by highlighting how Nazi sexism, which promoted an almost institutional lack of respect for women, in confluence with beliefs about Nazi racial superiority, facilitated sexual violence against Jewish women during the Holocaust.[26] Thus, over the course of two decades, historians established the validity of gender-based Holocaust studies.

More recently, historians have begun to focus their research specifically on Jewish women in the Holocaust, addressing the subject of sexual violence. It is important to note that historians tackling the subject are not unified in their approach and can be separated into two distinct groups. The first, although more prominent at the beginning of the 21st century, are those who conclude that there is little to no evidence of severe instances of sexual abuse against Jewish women, in particular rape, during the Holocaust. Historians adopting this position emphasize the importance of Nazi racial purity laws, and argue that to engage in sexual relations with a Jewish woman was considered the severe

---

[25] Dagmar Herzog, "Introduction", in *Sexuality and German Fascism*, 1-20.

[26] Monika Flaschka, "Rape, Race, and Gender in Nazi Occupied Territories," unpublished PhD Dissertation, Kent University State, 2009.

crime of *Rassenschande.* These scholars, including Dalia Ofer, Lenore Weitzman, Marlene Heinemann, Jack Morrison, and Sybil Milton argue that cases of rape were rare, however, they concede that Jewish women may have been terrorized by the *fear* of rape.[27] Along similar lines, Vera Laska contends that, "Rape was rare. While it is a fact that the SS could and did do as they pleased with any female inmate, raping them was not their preference. First of all, most of these women looked unattractive, without hair, dirty, smelly. Second, if caught in intercourse with a Jewish inmate, the SS were punished."[28] These scholars rely on the assumption that soldiers who violated the Nazi racial laws were harshly punished. Moreover, they presume that German men were largely committed to Nazi ideology, and therefore exercised "racially aware" sexual-restraint.[29] Lastly, they claim there is little evidence to indicate

---

[27] Dalia Ofer and Lenore J. Weitzman argue that because of German Racial policy incidences of rape were rare in, *Women in the Holocaust,* 7-8; Heinemann concedes that rape may have occurred, but emphasizes that the most universal form of abuse appears to have been verbal, in, *Gender and Destiny,* 16; Jack M. Morrison claims that Rassenchande laws were "overwhelmingly obeyed" in, *Ravensbruck: Everyday life in a Women's Concentration Camp, 1939-45,* 177-178. Historian Sybil Milton writes that the idea that Jewish women were forced to serve in SS brothels was a "popular postwar myth, sometimes exploited and sensationalized," and was "a macabre postwar misuse of the Holocaust for popular titillation." Sybil Milton, "Women and the Holocaust: The Case of German and German-Jewish Women," in *Different Voices: Women and the Holocaust,* ed. Carol Rittner and John K. Roth, 230-231.

[28] Vera Laska, "Women and the Holocaust: The Case of German and German Jewish Women," in *Different Voices,* 265.

[29] Regina Muhlhauser, "The Unquestioned Crime: Sexual Violence by German Soldiers during the War of Annihilation in the Soviet Union, 1941-1945," in *Rape in Wartime,* ed. Raphaelle Branche and Fabrice Virgili (New York: Palgrave Macmillan, 2012), 35.

sexual violence against Jewish women was widespread because it was not reported in *Rassenschande* cases.

In contrast, scholars such as Jonathon Friedman, Rochelle Saidel, Sonia Hedgepath, and Myrna Goldenberg reject the notion that laws forbidding *Rassenschande* prevented the rape of Jewish women, arguing instead that Nazi racial policy was not religiously adhered to nor uniformly followed.[30] They recognize sexual violence as an important component of Jewish women's Holocaust experience, arguing that sexual abuse, specifically rape, did indeed occur. More importantly, although sexual violence appears to contradict Nazi central policy, what previous scholars have failed to consider is that sexual violence dehumanizes and destroys its female victims, which in fact coincided with the Nazis' genocidal goals.[31]

---

[30] See, Jonathan Friedman, *Speaking the Unspeakable: Essays on Sexuality, Gender and Holocaust Survivor Memory* (Maryland, 2002), 54; Rochelle Saidel, *The Jewish Women of Ravensbruck Concentration Camp,* (Wisconsin: University of Wisconsin Press, 2004), 23; Myrna Goldenberg, "Sex, Rape and Survival: Jewish Women and the Holocaust," accessed online: *Women and the Holocaust: Scholarly Essays, http://www.theverylongview.com/WATH/,* (accessed, 16 May 2013).

[31] See especially, the groundbreaking publication of Sonja Hedgepeth and Rochelle Saidel's *Sexual Violence Against Jewish Women during the Holocaust,* (Massachusetts: Brandeis University Press, 2010). The book addresses various aspects of sexual violence, such as rape, forced prostitution, sexual humiliation, and sex for barter, and reveals that sexual violence not only occurred, but emphasizes that Nazi racial ideology did not constitute a barrier to sexual violence.

The problem of venturing into the matrix of sexual violence
in the context of the Holocaust is compounded by the lack of
precedents in Holocaust discourse and the limitation of statistical
data. Evidence, by and large, is found in survivor testimonies
and memoirs, rather than official documents. Friedman, Saidel,
Hedgepath, and Goldenberg, while recognizing the evidentiary
limitations and conceding that instances of rape and sexual
violence do not often appear in *Rassenschande* documents, believe
that oral testimonies and memoirs provide ample evidence of
sexual violence committed against Jewish women by Germans.
Indeed, as historian Elizabeth Baer has pointed out, "as scholars
read women's memoirs more extensively not only for what
they say, but also for what is coded and for elisions, and gaps,
we have detected much more sexual violence than had been
acknowledged,"[32] an important observation that casts both female
memoirs and testimonies in a new light.

Until these recent contributions, historians were apprehensive
to integrate stories of sexual violence into the sphere of traditional
survivor experiences and silence was deemed preferable to opposing
the taboo against talking about the subject. With innumerable victims
and immeasurable quantities of suffering, historians approached sexual
violence in a cursory manner, regarding it as a natural byproduct of
genocide, and yet too horrifying for thorough analysis. Moreover,
many historians felt uncomfortable and unsure of how to examine
such events. For example, Holocaust historian Joan Ringelheim, a
pioneer in the field of women and the Holocaust, explains that during

---

[32]   Elizabeth Baer, "Rereading Women's Holocaust Memoirs: Liana Milli's
Smoke Over Birkenau," in *Lessons and Legacies VIII*, 162-63.

the interviews she conducted in the 1980's, she was uncertain how to approach the subject of sexual violence. In one interview in particular, a Jewish woman admitted that a German man had raped her. Ringelheim concedes to not knowing how to handle the remainder of the interview and explains, "I believe we avoid listening because we are afraid; sometimes we avoid listening because we don't understand the importance of what is being said. Without a place for a particular memory, without a conceptual framework, a possibly significant piece of information will not be pursued."[33]

There was also a tendency to treat matters pertaining to sexual violence during the Holocaust as either too trivial, uncomfortable, or potentially too inappropriately titillating for systematic study. Many feared, rather than deepening our understanding of the Holocaust, the study of sexual violence might simultaneously disgust and titillate the reader, making the Holocaust, in an perverse way, sexually stimulating.[34] Arguably, however, by analyzing the sexual violence against Jewish women during the Holocaust, an event charged with utter intensity, a greater understanding of wider historical perspectives can be achieved.[35]

Another significant barrier to the study of sexual violence was survivors' reluctance to publically testify to having been raped, or sexually abused, fearing it would invite moral judgment, and bring shame, embarrassment and dishonor to themselves and

---

[33]   Joan Ringelheim, "The Split Between Gender and the Holocaust," in *Women in the Holocaust,* 342.

[34]   Dagmar Herzog, *Sexuality and German Fascism,* 55.

[35]   John K. Roth, "Equality, Neutrality, Particularity," in, *Experience and Expression,* ed., Baer and Goldenberg, 13.

their families. Victims were apprehensive to speak of experiences that lie outside the traditional female victimization narrative; an absence which has undoubtedly inhibited other witnesses who experienced sexual abuse from coming forward. Moreover, because of the importance scholars have placed on German racial purity laws, and the skepticism surrounding the legitimacy of survivor testimony, many victims feared their stories of sexual violence would not be heard.[36] Placing the burden of proof on survivors has thus effectively silenced many of them.

As a result of recent studies, however, historians today are asking new questions of their sources and interviewees. Most recently, historians have begun to confront the issues surrounding the study of sexual violence, overcoming enduring taboos. This new line of inquiry is creating an atmosphere in which female survivors are now freer to share stories that are uncomfortable for historians and survivors alike. This simultaneously coincides with two other factors: spouses dying, and an increasing acceptance of oral testimony and memoirs as historical evidence. In many cases, once the spouses of female victims were deceased, the victims became more willing to discuss issues of sexual violence. Moreover, historians have largely accepted survivor testimony and memoirs as a rich source of evidence that as long as critically evaluated and held to the same empirical standards as all other historical

---

[36] For example, Meili Steele contends that many survivors have been criticized for not adhering to historical facts, and suggests that putting the burden of proof on survivors has led to their silencing and marginalization, in, "The Reliability of Survivor Narratives of the Holocaust" in *History in Dispute,* 4-5.

sources, are considered equally as valuable as official documents. Many have also recognized that by focusing exclusively on official documentation, crucial aspects of the Holocaust, namely the reality of the victims' experiences, would otherwise remain hidden.

In light of these recent developments and the increasing awareness of survivor testimony, this study is capable of pushing the line of inquiry further forward and building upon the work of Saidel, Friedman, Goldenberg, and Hedgepath to argue that despite the existence of laws forbidding *Rassenschande,* Jewish women experienced sexual violence at the hands of the Nazis. This study will also reveal that Jewish women not only experienced sexual violence, but this sexual violence was an integral aspect of the Nazi machinery of destruction. Moreover, the functions of sexual violence for its perpetrators and the ways in which sex both motivated them and enabled them to commit genocide will be fully illuminated in all its complex dimensions.

Methodology

Writing on a topic considered to be "taboo" and marginal is fraught with difficulties, which are compounded by the limitation of existing "official" documentation.[37] This lack of "official" evidence

---

[37]   "Official" documentation consists of sources generated at the time by institutions of the Nazi State, including, the German Army High Command records, Reich Security Main Office records, Einsatzgruppen reports, files from Krupp, Henschel, and other German industrial concerns, Luftwaffe material, records kept by Heinrich Himmler, German Foreign Office records, the courts, and many others.

has made it difficult to establish that Jewish women experienced sexual violence, and has undoubtedly contributed to the absence of discourse around the subject. In light of these limitations, it is essential to adopt a broad geographical scope and to utilize a wide variety of sources including published memoirs, and testimonies to fill out the picture of this underexamined topic. As a result of the lack of scholarship in this arena of study, it was not feasible, nor fruitful, to undertake a micro-study of one specific location in Europe. This study therefore includes instances of sexual violence from various countries across Eastern Europe. Moreover, this study examines incidents of sexual violence against Jewish women in various settings including the Eastern territories, camps, ghettos, and brothels, which demonstrates that sexual violence was widespread during the Holocaust, and was not an isolated phenomenon. Thus, by examining sexual violence within a broad contextual and geographical framework, this study can accentuate the similarities or differences between instances of sexual violence perpetrated across the historical borders, and attempt to find a unifying link between the instances and functions of sexual violence during the Holocaust.

In the absence of official documentation, the narratives of survivors are the primary body of evidence available to reveal instances of sexual violence against Jewish women during the Holocaust. To downplay the significance of these sources is to downplay the magnitude of sexual horrors these women experienced. Thus, working on the assumption that survivor testimony, though flawed, offers certain insights, this study draws on a wide range of published and unpublished testimonies. These include memoirs written by survivors shortly after liberation as well as those written in more recent years. Rather than accepting memoirs as transparent documents of the horrors they discuss, this study applies the same methodological scrutiny to memoirs as Myrna Goldenberg and Elizabeth Baer's anthology, *Experience and Expression: Women, the Nazis, and the Holocaust.* Their study differs from its predecessors by examining the uses of women's Holocaust memoirs by scholars, arguing that although fraught with difficulties, the use of memoirs is acceptable. In the essay included in this volume, Pascale Bos argues that much of the first-generation research on the Holocaust and women did not examine how Holocaust narratives related to reality, with many early scholars accepting narratives as trustworthy sources.[38] This early uncritical acceptance allowed for many faulty assumptions to be made, which in turn caused many scholars to shun memoirs as an acceptable source.[39] This study therefore undertakes a critical acceptance of narratives by acknowledging that any source can contain incorrect details, however, small details are less problematic if numerous testimonies contain similar content. What is more important is the overall pattern and key points that survivor narratives provide,

---

[38] Pascale Rachel Bos, "Women and the Holocaust: Analyzing Gender Difference," in *Experience and Expression: Women the Nazis, and the Holocaust,* 29.

[39] On the uncritical acceptance and misuse of memoirs see Ruth Franklin, *A Thousand Darknesses: Lies and Truth in Holocaust Fiction* (Oxford University Press, 2010). Franklin argues that until recently, Holocaust memoirs were guaranteed an uncritical acceptance, which allowed for many faulty assumptions to be made by readers. In particular, Franklin discusses the influential memoir, *Fragments,* by Binjamin Wilkomirski, which within a few years was determined to be a fraud. Franklin, however, does not discount the value of memoirs; rather she contends that Holocaust scholars must place primary emphasis on establishing evidence—facts, proof—rather than on literary and aesthetic representation.

which are supplemented by contextual research and other forms of evidence, including oral testimonies. In essays by Susan Nowak and Catherine Bernand, they problematize the use of memoirs, calling on scholars to recognize narratives as constructions and reconstructions of individual experiences and memories.[40] In a related way, Zoe Waxman's recent book, *Writing the Holocaust,* calls attention to the problematic representation of women's Holocaust testimonies. Waxman argues that testimonies tend to focus on the desire to fulfill traditional gendered expectations, resulting in testimonies that are constructed to fulfill pre-existing gender ideals.[41] There is also a tendency amongst historians to ignore 'difficult' testimonies, which reveal experiences outside the traditional female Holocaust narrative. These contentions, such as the reliability of survivor testimony and their problematic uses by historians, have raised important issues in contemporary discussions in Holocaust studies about the uses and value of

---

[40]   See, Susan Nowack, "Ruptured Lives and Shattered Beliefs: A Feminist Analysis of *Tikkun Atzmi* in Holocaust Literature," in *Experience and Expression: Women the Nazis, and the Holocaust,* 180-201. Nowack examines the ways in which female writers use their own memoirs to construct their desired identities in the post-Holocaust world.
See, also, Catherine Bernard, "Anne Frank: The Cultivation of the Inspirational Victim," in *Experience and Expression: Women the Nazis, and the Holocaust,* 201-228. Bernard examines the ways in which Anne Frank's diary has been misused, improperly translated, and textually abused.

[41]   Zoe Waxman, *Writing the Holocaust: Identity, Testimony, Representation* (Oxford: Oxford University Press, 2006), 138. The 'traditional' Jewish experience and 'traditional' female identity are constructed on the basis of roles such as 'mother', 'caregiver', 'daughter', 'nurturer', and testimonies are often selected on the basis of whether or not they reinforce these pre-existing ideas.

memoirs and testimonies. Most importantly for the study at hand, the contentions raised concerning the characteristics, specifically credibility, that distinguish the testimonies and memoirs published in different periods following the Holocaust.[42]

The primary focus of this study is on the earlier memoirs written between 1945 and 1960, mainly by female Jewish survivors from Europe. The research emphasis on memoirs from this period is intentional, as survivor recollections from this period were less influenced by reading the memoirs of others, or reading historical, psychological, and sociological research on the Holocaust. Also, they were written before survivors were exposed to what constituted the "traditional" female experience. Most importantly, they were written before the survivor's memory was "shaped,"[43] and influenced by a desire to fulfill or make their experiences compatible with traditional gendered expectations. Na'ama Shik contends that early memoirs were written with less restraint, often vividly describing Nazi sadism, which expressed itself in sexual violence. This early openness about sexual violence, Shik argues,

---

[42] Adopted from Na'ama Shik's study, "Infinite Loneliness: Some aspects of the Lives of Jewish Women in the Auschwitz Camps According to Testimonies and Autobiographies Written Between 1945 and 1948" in *Lessons and Legacies VIII: From Generation to Generation*. ed., Peter Hayes and Doris L. Bergen (Northwestern University Press, 2008). The various memoirs and testimony publications can be divided into four chronological waves: the first published between 1945 and 1948; the second between 1952 and 1970; the third between 1970 and 1980; and the fourth between the 1980's and continues to today.

[43] For an explanation on how survivor memories are "shaped" and influenced by others, see Joan Ringelheim, "The Split between Gender and the Holocaust," in *Women in the Holocaust*.

was not yet tainted by the reaction of the post-war world, which would later engage in "blaming the victim."[44]

Although I emphasize the value of this early corpus of memoirs, they are not the only important sources for tracing the history of sexual violence against Jewish women. In order to obtain the most complete picture as possible, memoirs from subsequent periods are also examined, in an effort to demonstrate that incidences of sexual violence are indeed in evidence. In some cases, survivors needed many years before they were able to speak or write about instances of sexual abuse. By distancing themselves from the event, they were able to come to terms with and share what they had experienced.[45]

Continually, since sexual violence does not fit neatly within the traditional Holocaust victimization narrative, when survivors do address sexual violence in interviews and memoirs, it is often done so in a covert manner, offered with little detail, echoing their guilt and shame.[46] Recognizing this, this study has detected much more sexual violence than has been previously acknowledged

---

[44] Na'ama Shik, "Sexual Abuse of Jewish Women in Auschwitz-Birkenau," in *Brutality and Desire: War and Sexuality in Europe's Twentieth Century,* ed. Dagmar Herzog (New York: Palgrave Macmillan, 2009) 221-46.

[45] For example, Jewish survivor, Fanya Gottesfeld Heller waited fifty years before testifying that a Gestapo man had raped her aunt right in front of her. See, Fanya Gottesfeld Heller, *Love In A World Of Sorrow: A Teenage Girl's Holocaust Memoirs* (Devora Publishing, 2005), 81.

[46] Sonja M. Hedgepeth and Rochelle G. Saidel, "Introduction," in *Sexual Violence Against Jewish Women during the Holocaust,* ed., Sonja M. Hedgepeth and Rochelle G. Saidel, 2.

by examining women's memoirs not only for what they say, but also for what is inferred, and coded. Moreover, sexual violence may constitute something different for each victim. Particular acts of violence or humiliation that some survivors may interpret as having no sexual component could be perceived as an act of sexual violence by others. Survivor memoirs are therefore re-read, re-examined, and sometimes re-interpreted to identify previously overlooked experiences, that for the victim, constituted an event of sexual violence.[47] Thus, if a survivor identifies a particular incident as having a sexual component, regardless of historians that do not categorize such event as sexual violence, this study accepts the self-assessment of the survivor.

Another important body of evidence comes from survivor oral testimonies. In order to establish the fact that the rarity of descriptions of sexual violence in published memoirs should not be interpreted as evidence that sexual violence did not occur, this study also consulted forty unpublished oral testimonies from the Shoah Foundation Oral History Archives. Composed of over 52,000 testimonies, this collection is the largest audio video collection of Holocaust testimonies in the world. These testimonies were of particular importance to this study, as the interviewer asked the survivors if they had witnessed sexual abuse. Among

---

[47] For example, in women's memoirs, the forced nudity upon entry into the camps is often interpreted differently, with some survivors describing it as a trauma of sexual violence while others interpret it as story of vulnerability in that it involves nudity in front of SS men. See, Kirsty Chatwood, "Re-Interpreting Stories of Sexual Violence: The Multiple Testimonies of Lucille Eichengreen," in *Life, Death and Sacrifice: Women and Family in the Holocaust* ed. Esther Hertzog (New York: Gefen, 2008), 163-164.

the 52,000 interviews conducted, 2,650 testimonies reference rape and sexual molestation, and more than one thousand of these testimonies explicitly state that the victim of sexual violence was Jewish. At first glance this number may appear to be relatively small, however, these testimonies of sexual violence amount to roughly two percent of the total 52,000 Holocaust testimonies. If this percentage is extrapolated and applied to the roughly 6 million Jewish victims of the Holocaust, approximately 120,000 Jewish victims experienced sexual violence, a number that is clearly not insignificant. It must also be noted that no study of testimony can be completely representative of the victims of the Holocaust, as a majority of Jews perished without ever writing down their experiences. Moreover, as Auschwitz survivor Judith Magyar Isaacson reminds us: "The Anne Franks who survived rape don't tell their stories."[48] Significantly, however, a majority of the Shoah Foundation oral interviews were conducted in the late 1990's, after the spouses of many of the female victims were deceased, which, in some cases made them more willing to discuss such issues. Most importantly, oral testimonies can reveal more than just historical facts of the Holocaust. As historian Caroline Schaumann argues, survivor testimonies reveal something fundamental about the nature of the Holocaust that cannot be conveyed through other historical documentation.[49]

---

[48]   Judith Magyar Isaacson, *Seed of Sarah: Memoirs of a Survivor* (Illinois: University of Illinois Press, 1990), 144.

[49]   Caroline Schaumann, "The Reliability of Survivor Narratives of the Holocaust," in *History in Dispute, Vol. 11: The Holocaust, 1933-1945.* ed., Benjamin Frankel, (St. James Press, 1999).

This study also draws on the published oral interviews conducted by American psychologist David Boder in "Displaced Persons" camps in 1946. Boder interviewed over one hundred and thirty displaced persons, beginning in late July 1946, making these interviews among the earliest recordings of Holocaust survivors. As of late 2009, all of Boder's 1946 interviews were transcribed and translated, made fully available to the public through *The Voices of the Holocaust Project* online website. 50 Although only one testimony in this collection has been used for the study, the uncensored nature of the Jewish female survivor's discussion on rape is further proof that incidences of sexual violence are, in fact, in evidence.

From the large body of testimonies and memoirs examined, all of which discuss sexual abuse and rape, it is evident that sexual violence against women during the Holocaust is not a hidden history, but a history that scholars have only recently acknowledged. By combining previously published memoirs with rarely accessed unpublished testimonies this study reveals patterns of sexual violence which span across geographical and institutional boundaries. Sexual violence against Jewish women occurred in the Eastern territories, in ghettos, in brothels, and in labour and concentration camps. It was perpetrated by members of the SS, Einsatzgruppen, and Wehrmacht. This body of evidence confirms the assertions made by historians like Saidel, Friedman, and Goldenberg, who argue that German men committed sexual violence against Jewish women despite *Rassenschande* laws

---

50   See, http://voices.iit.edu/voices_project.

expressly prohibiting it. Furthermore, not only did it happen, this violence was, in fact, widespread.

In my investigation into acts of sexual violence during the Holocaust, I have deliberately confined myself to the examination of Jewish women only. This means that I do not examine the experiences of non-Jewish men or women, nor do I examine the experiences of Jewish men. My concentration upon Jewish women is not intended to diminish the indignities suffered by all others victims of the Holocaust, as the acknowledgement of gender differences does not in any way imply greater victimization, rather this narrow focus is meant to highlight the particular vulnerability of Jewish women; what historian Judith Baumel calls "double jeopardy."[51]

As previously established, both Jewish women and men were victims of sexual violence during the Holocaust, however, by virtue of their biology, Jewish women were vulnerable to victimization connected to female sexuality and endured experiences that Jewish men could not.[52] Ideological notions of

---

[51] See Judith Tydor Baumel, *Double Jeopardy: Gender and the Holocaust* (London: Vallentine Mitchell, 1998). Baumel argues that Jewish women were persecuted as both Jews and women during the Holocaust. They were first the victims of Nazi racial theory and secondly the victims of Nazi sexism and misogyny.

[52] I am not suggesting that men do not have equally unique experiences because of their sex. Jewish men also endured specific experiences as a result of their biological differences. For example, circumcision made Jewish men easily identifiable, and hence, particularly vulnerable. See, Sara Horowitz, "Women in Holocaust literature: Engendering Trauma Memory," in *Women in the Holocaust,* 365.

gender informed the process and policies of annihilation, and Jewish women were seen as both sexual objects, and a biological threat, as carriers of the next generation of "vengeful" Jews.[53] In the enforcement of their racist goals, the Nazis subjected Jewish women to various forms of sexual violence—forced abortion, forced sterilization, "medical" experiments—intent on controlling Jewish women's sexuality and their reproductive abilities. Also important, fewer Jewish women attained positions of power in the ghettos and camps. Their status-or lack of status—compounded their vulnerability to sexual exploitation by men in positions of power, particularly German authorities and concentration camp inmates with special privileges.[54] Jewish women therefore bore a unique double burden as women and Jews, suffering from antisemitism and sexism in their genocidal forms.[55] Thus, although the threat of sexual violence was universal and constituted one of the most horrific traumas for men and women, Jewish women's lives were frequently very different from those of Jewish men, necessitating the study of women's particular experiences.

By examining the nature of sexual violence in all its complex dimensions, this study sits at an intersection of several topics, and is influenced by and contributes to multiple historiographical themes, including: women and the Holocaust, German sexuality,

---

[53] Joan Ringelheim, "Thoughts about Women in the Holocaust," in *Thinking the Unthinkable,* ed. Roger S. Gottlieb (New York: Paulist Press, 1990), 147.

[54] It must be noted that sex in exchange for survival was sometimes part of the male experience, however it does not feature as prominently in the historical record.

[55] Joan Ringelheim, "Thoughts About Women and the Holocaust," in *Thinking the Unthinkable: Meanings of the Holocaust,* 147.

the intersection of gender and racial ideology under Nazism, and more specifically, the functions of sexual violence in wartime. By applying discursive analysis to an oral and memoir source base, sexual violence can be understood as a subject of intrinsic importance. It sheds light not only on the matter of sexual violence during the Holocaust, but the ideological character of Nazism and the diverse functions that sexual violence served for its perpetrators. Most importantly, this study reveals that Jewish women did indeed experience sexual violence at the hands of the Germans and this violence became an integral part of the process of annihilation in the Third Reich.

SECTION 2

INSTANCES AND FUNCTIONS OF SEXUAL VIOLENCE

Sexual violence occurs in peacetime, but in the context of war and genocide, this phenomenon multiplies and the number of cases increases drastically.[56] Rape flourishes in warfare irrespective of geographic location or nationality and has long been considered as a natural byproduct of armed conflicts wherein the victors rape the women of the vanquished.[57] War creates an atmosphere that intensifies the brutality, repetitiveness, and probability of rape by diminishing men's sensitivity to human suffering, and intensifying innate sexual instincts.[58] For the perpetrators, who often harbor different ideas about sexuality, gender, race, and violence, the motivation to commit sexual violence is not monolithic. The prevailing theoretical explanations concerning the

---

[56] Sonja M. Hedgepeth and Rochelle G. Saidel, "Introduction," in *Sexual Violence against Women during the Holocaust*, 13.

[57] Susan Brownmiller, *Against our Will: Men, Women and Rape* (New York: Simon and Schuster, 1975), 32.

[58] Lois Ann Lorentzen and Jennifer Turpin, ed., *Women and War Reader* (New York: New York University Press, 1998) 76.

causes of wartime rape contend that rape in war is not incidental but functional, serving a larger purpose than itself. Sociocultural factors are instrumental in shaping perpetrator motivation, as well as biological factors such as the sexual desire of the individual soldiers.[59] Sexual violence during war is, however, not only an expression of sexuality. It is an expression of violence committed via sexuality. It should be understood as a show of power on the part of the perpetrator and a demonstration of dominance and superiority through the degradation and dehumanization of the victim.[60]

In the context of the Holocaust, sexual violence against Jewish women was both unique and typical. It was typical in the forms that sexual violence manifested-sexual humiliation, rape, gang rape, sexual slavery-but unique in the patterns it followed and the functions it served for the Nazi regime. Moreover, sexual violence during the Holocaust was not a strategy of war, nor a state-sanctioned policy from above; it evolved into a byproduct of the dehumanization process of genocide. Genocidal conditions created a fertile atmosphere for sexual violence to occur, and as Omer Bartov notes, "conditions of omnipresent murder attracts and breeds sadists."[61] Continually, these conditions not only intensify the brutality, and repetitiveness of sexual violence but as noted

---

[59] Jonathan Gottschall, "Explaining Wartime Rape." *The Journal of Sex Research,* Vol. 41, No. 2 (May 2004): 134.

[60] Brigitte Halbmayr, "Sexualized Violence Against Women during Nazi "Racial" Persecution, in *Sexual Violence against Jewish Women during the Holocaust,* 30.

[61] Omer Bartov, *Germany's War and the Holocaust: Disputed Holocaust,* (Cornell: Cornell University Press, 2003), 104.

by numerous scholars, diminish the perpetrators "sensitivity to suffering and intensifies men's sense of entitlement, superiority, avidity, and social license to rape."[62]

In order to effectively approach this complex study, and to understand the meaning of sexual violence during the Third Reich, it is essential to provide a framework which not only defines sexual violence, but also establishes its nature, constituents and diverse functions in the particular system of mass death. I therefore propose a broad definition of sexual violence during the Holocaust, because to focus only on extreme forms of sexual abuse runs the risk of marginalizing other forms of sexual violence to which even greater numbers of Jewish women may have been subjected. These forms of sexual violence include sexual humiliation, sexual slavery, rape, and gang rape. By adopting a definition that encompasses a wide range of sexual abuses, and allows for the inclusion of both direct and indirect expressions of sexual violence, the most productive and thorough analysis can be achieved.

First, sexual humiliation can be understood as a form of sexual violence because through this form of violence, women are stripped of their humanity and female identity in a barrage of indignities, specifically the infringement of their intimate space. Many Nazi perpetrators gained a sense of arousal and erotic excitement through the sexual humiliation of Jewish women, particularly, their forced nudity. Second, sexual slavery, in particular camp prostitution, is an institutionalized and

---

[62]   Rhonda Copelon, as quoted in, Ann Barstow, ed., *War's Dirty Secret: Rape, Prostitution and other Crimes Against Women* (Cleveland: Pilgrim Press, 2000), 8.

therefore sanctioned form of sexual violence. In the context of the Holocaust, Jewish women were held against their will and forced to engage in sexual relations with not only the German perpetrators, but also their fellow victims. Lastly, rape, as a violent invasion of one's body that attacks the intimate self and dignity of a human being, must be seen as a severe and often deadly form of sexual violence.[63] During the Holocaust, Jewish women experienced rape in a variety of forms, specifically, private rapes, gang rapes, and public rapes. Bearing these categories in mind, the diverse and unique functions of sexual violence during the Holocaust must also be established.

During the Holocaust, the motivation to perpetrate sexual violence was not monolithic, and always served a diversity of functions. Sometimes sexual violence was a means for the perpetrators to assert their power, and sometimes it was a form of male bonding, wherein abusing their victims was a means of entertaining each other. Other times it was meant to dehumanize the victims while simultaneously brutalizing and desensitizing the perpetrator. And in some cases sexual violence was meant to reward and satisfy sexual urges. What becomes horrifyingly clear, as this study argues, is that Jewish women experienced sexual violence during the Holocaust, and that violence was both a necessary and instrumental component of the continuing functioning of genocide.

---

[63] Ruth Seifert, *Gender Dynamics and Post-Conflict Reconstruction,* (New York: Peter Lang, 2009).

I will examine instances of four forms of sexual violence: humiliation, sexual slavery, rape and gang rape within the framework of the functions these acts performed: sexual satisfaction, masculine ego gratification, humiliation and dehumanization. It is often the case that more than one form of sexual violence can be engaged to fulfill a particular function. For example, sexual satisfaction was achieved through rape and sexual slavery. Finally, these instances and functions of sexual violence will be examined across geographical boundaries. These acts occurred in the Eastern occupied territories, ghettos, brothels, and labour and concentration camps.

Functions of Sexual Violence

In the Third Reich, sexual violence against Jewish women took many forms, which manifested in a diversity of contexts. In the Eastern Occupied territories, Jewish women, either before death or deportation to camps, experienced widespread sexual violence. Upon internment, within ghettos and concentration camps, Jewish women also experienced extensive instances of sexual violence. And lastly, within the confines of the Nazi institutionalized brothels, Jewish women experienced daily instances of sexual violence. Thus, in order to effectively analyze these abuses, and attempt to understand how sexual violence became an integral part of the genocidal process, instances of sexual violence and the contexts in which they occurred, will be examined according to their function. These functions can be divided into four categories: sexual satisfaction, masculine ego gratification, sexual humiliation and dehumanization. These divisions are not intended to draw clear-cut lines between the identified functions of sexual violence, as these functions are not mutually exclusive. Sexual violence may be motivated by and serve many functions, and in some instances, almost all of the categorized factors materialize, interact and overlap with one another. Thus, although, these divisions are far from definitive, they serve as a useful starting point to methodically examine the motivation to perpetrate sexual violence and the function this violence served for its perpetrators.

In addition, examples of each of these functions will be examined within the following four contexts: The Eastern occupied territories, ghettos, brothels, and labor and concentration camps. It is important to note that each of these contexts gave rise to different conditions in which the acts of sexual violence occurred. In the East, sexual violence was perpetrated across vast boundaries, and in the context of a war of annihilation. In this wartime atmosphere of omnipresent death, perpetrators were deeply dependent on each other, and became largely inured and desensitized to violence against Jews. This, in combination with the Eastern military leadership's lenient stance towards *Rassenschande,* created fertile conditions for sexual violence to occur.[64] In the ghettos, unlike the eastern territories, perpetrators were safe and protected from the horrors of war. Moreover, Jewish women were confined to spaces where they lived for long periods

---

[64]   See, for instance, Regina Muhlhauser, "The Unquestioned Crime: Sexual Violence by German Soldiers during the War of Annihilation in the Soviet Union, 1941-1945," in *Rape in Wartime,* 40-43. Muhlhauser argues that in the East, most military commanders deemed sexual violence to be a normal, and unavoidable aspect of war. Moreover, because male virility was presumed to be an expression of masculinity and strength, most military commanders did not strictly enforce the bans on sexual contact with "inferior" races.

of time under the watchful eye of both German and civilian authorities, which facilitated sexual violence of a more clandestine nature. In labor and concentration camps, Jewish women were also forcibly interned, however, the dynamics in the Nazi camp situation gave rise to different instances of sexual violence. The Nazi camps were places where perpetrators worked day after day amidst the corpses of murdered human beings, and these men had total power over the life and death of their Jewish prisoners. This combination did much to turn the camps into laboratories of unbridled sexual exploitation. Lastly, within the context of the brothel system, the particular nature of sexual violence also differed; manifesting itself in the form of state sanctioned and institutionalized sexual slavery. Thus, through these divisions, the subsequent chapter will argue that sexual violence against Jewish women not only happened but was extensive. It will also reveal the ways in which sexual violence ultimately became part of the process of annihilation in the Third Reich.

CHAPTER 1
SEXUAL VIOLENCE FOR SEXUAL PLEASURE

During the Third Reich, Jewish women experienced sexual violence throughout the Nazi-Occupied territories both before their internment into ghettos and camps, and once they were confined to such spaces. For the perpetrator, the motivation to commit sexual violence was not uniform. To varying degrees they were motivated by a desire to humiliate, and dehumanize their victims, to increase their sense of power and camaraderie, and by a desire for sexual pleasure. For every instance of sexual abuse, the motivational factors varied, with some factors being more prominent than others and multiple factors often motivating the same act of sexual violence. The variations were largely dependent on the time, and context in which the violation occurred, and the individual perpetrator's goals. In many instances of sexual violence, a powerful motivation seems to have been the desire to fulfill sexual urges, especially in the context of the Nazi camp brothels. Although some rape theorists argue that rape has nothing to do with sexual desire, it is evident from the variety of sources examined that instances of sexual violence, from rape to sexual slavery, and gang rape, were different manifestations of sexual desire, lying on a continuum of violence.[65]

The Eastern Occupied Territories

Amidst the brutal war in Eastern Europe, rape was regularly employed as a means for perpetrators to achieve sexual satisfaction, which many believed was a "traditional" soldier's reward during war. Despite the official military rules and racial laws against miscegenation, German men-members of the Wehrmacht, the SS, and the Police—regularly raped Jewish women. Nazi anti-Jewish practice and law varied significantly based on location and leadership, and as a result, what took place during the war in the East did not always match the directed racial policy.[66] On the whole, Nazi authorities were aware of the sexual abuses occurring, and silently accepted these forms of sexual violence as an unavoidable product of brutal warfare.[67] And when

---

[65] See for example, Ruth Seifert, "War and Rape: A Preliminary Analysis," in *Mass Rape: The War Against Women in Bosnia-Herzegovina*, ed. Alexandra Stiglmayer (Lincoln and London: University of Nebraska Press, 1994). Seifert argues that, "rape is not an aggressive manifestation of sexuality, but rather a sexual manifestation of aggression. In the perpetrator's psyche it serves no sexual purpose but is the expression of rage, violence, and dominance over a woman." 84.

[66] Helene Sinnreich, "And it was something we didn't talk about:" Rape of Jewish Women During the Holocaust." *Holocaust Studies: A Journal of Culture and History*, Vol. 14, No.2, Autumn 2008, 1-22.

[67] Regina Muhlhauser, "Between 'Racial Awareness' and Fantasies of Potency: Nazi Sexual Politics in the Occupied Territories of the Soviet Union, 1942-1945," in *Sexual Violence Against Jewish Women during the Holocaust,* 203.

laws of racial purity were in fact broken, there was little to no punishment.[68] According to Omer Bartov, sexual crimes against the civilian populations in the East were rarely punished because they "constituted a convenient safety valve for venting the men's anger and frustration caused by the rigid discipline demanded from men and by the increasingly heavy cost . . . of the war."[69] Sexual violence against Jewish women in this ideological war of annihilation was, to some degree, seen as justified and an apparently necessary outlet for satisfying male sexual urges and releasing tensions produced by war.[70]

Sexual violence against Jewish women in the East must therefore be understood as a routine part of the process of exploitation and murder, wherein the perpetrators were largely motivated by a desire for sexual pleasure. Various reports and testimonies discuss countless cases of rape and sexual violations, wherein the youngest, most beautiful Jewish women are selected to fulfill the sexual desires of the German men. As one testimony from a Polish doctor in Warsaw attests, "One continually hears of the raping of Jewish girls in Warsaw. In one mirror shop on Swietojerska Street there was a mass raping of Jewish girls. The Germans seized the most beautiful and most healthy girls on the

---

[68] Birgit Beck, "Rape: The Military Trials of Sexual Crimes Committed by Soldiers in the Wehrmacht, 1939-1944," in *Home Front: The Military, War, and Gender in Twentieth Century Germany,* ed., Karen Hagemann and Stefanie Schueler-Springorum (Oxford: Berg, 2000), 263.

[69] Omer Bartov, *Hitler's Army. Soldiers, Nazis and the War in the Third Reich.* (New York: Oxford University Press, 1991), 61.

[70] Birgit Beck, "Rape: The Military Trials of Sexual Crimes Committed by Soldiers in the Wehrmacht, 1939-1944," in *Home Front: The Military, War, and Gender in Twentieth Century Germany.* 265-266.

streets . . . the girls were raped."[71] In this episode of rape, where the perpetrators engaged in sexual activity with Jewish women who were both young and beautiful, it would seem implausible to argue that raping had nothing to do with the perpetrators' sexual desires. Although abuse of power is also evident here, the fact that the perpetrators selected their victims specifically based on their attractiveness reveals a primary motivation for sexual pleasure.

Jewish survivor Frieda Frome reports several instances of sexual violence in her memoir, *Some Dare to Dream,* stating that German men were very willing to break racial laws to engage in sex. In Lithuania, Frome explains, German officers would select attractive young Jewish women to live in their apartments, almost all of whom were eventually murdered once the perpetrator grew tired of them.[72] Survivor Anna Dychkant tells interviewer Father Patrick Desbois of similar occurrences in Busk, Ukraine: "The young Jewish girls-there was one who went to school with me, Silvia, who were very beautiful-they weren't killed straight away. Silvia had to live with the German commander. The other girls waited on the other soldiers. When the girls got pregnant they were killed."[73] According to Anton Davidovski, another witness interviewed by Father Patrick Desbois, the Germans forced the

---

[71] Jacob Apenszlak, ed. *The Black Book of Polish Jewry: An Account of Martyrdom of Polish Jewry.* (New York: Roy Publishers, 1943), 29.

[72] Frieda Frome, *Some Dare to Dream* (Iowa: Iowa University Press, 1988), 64-68.

[73] Father Patrick Desbois. *The Holocaust by Bullets* (New York: Palgrave Macmillan, 2008), 85. In 2004, in the Ukraine and Belarus, Father Patrick Desbois began interviewing witnesses to the Jewish massacres of 1941 and 1943. He compiled the interviews into the work, *The Holocaust by Bullets.*

most beautiful Jewish girls to work in the offices of the Gestapo where they were kept as sexual slaves.[74] The fact that the beauty of the victims is always noted in these examples indicates that these women were not randomly chosen, but rather, that they were deliberately chosen for their beauty. Selecting women for their attractiveness further supports the notion that the perpetrators in these instances were primarily motivated by sexual desire as opposed to power, masculine ego gratification, or the desire to humiliate.

Irene Binzer, a Jewish survivor who was captured and confined to a prison outside Belgrade after the Germans invaded Yugoslavia in April of 1941, attests to similar cases of sexual slavery. In the prison, Binzer was held in a solitary confinement cell for over a year, and kept as the personal sex slave of a German official. She testifies, "he had a key [to the cell] and he was the only one who had a key. He raped me over and over and over again."[75] The German raped her at least once a day and was the only man who raped her in the prison. What is most telling about Binzer's testimony is that over time, the German began talking to Binzer during his daily visits, telling her about his personal life, including his wife and children. The German did not want to kill Binzer himself and eventually transferred her and her mother from the prison after a year. In such a scenario, where the perpetrator rapes his victim on a daily basis, in private, and with no gratuitous violence, sexual satisfaction can be understood as a primary motivator. The fact that Binzer became a sexual as well as

---

[74]   Desbois, *Holocaust by Bullets,* 85.

[75]   Irene Binzer, Interview Code 28053, USC Shoah Foundation Institute.

emotional outlet for the German also highlights the ways in which sex could function as a release for the tensions produced by war.

The perpetrators' motivation to satisfy sexual urges is most evident in cases where the victims are forced to engage in a wide range of sexual acts, from oral sex, to vaginal sex, and urolagnia.[76] In the testimony of two Polish Jewish women, they discuss the mass rape of women from Vilnus, Lithuania. They explain in rather explicit language that German men told young Jewish girls to, "take the sexual organs into their mouths and suck as they would suck their mother's breast. And they were told to swallow and imagine that this was honey or milk. They tied a twelve-year-old girls to a bench, and six Germans and six Lithuanians finished the sexual acts twice each."[77] Next, the perpetrators selected another set of Jewish girls for rape and finished their sexual deed by ejaculating and urinating on the victims' faces.[78] The fact that these men gave their victims detailed instructions to follow and forced them to engage in multiple forms of sexual activity selected based on their individual desires, supports the notion that this was an act of sexual satisfaction. Such episodes of sexual violence reveal the ways in which the perpetrators sexually violated Jewish girls as a means to not only fulfill their sexual desires but also their perverse sexual fantasies.

---

[76] Urolagnia is a sexual activity where people gain sexual pleasure from urine and/or urination during sexual intercourse.

[77] USHMMA, RG-06.025*01 RIGA N-18313, tom 18, doc. 117, as cited in, Wendy Jo Gertjejanssen, "Victims, Heroes, Survivors," unpublished PhD. Dissertation, University of Minnesota, 2004.

[78] Ibid.

Labor and Concentration Camps

Similar cases are reported in labor and concentration camps. For example, in Felicia Karay's study of forced-labor camps in the Radom district of Poland, Karay describes the camps as a place where the "rites of manhood" were expressed in the orgies and gang rapes of Jewish girls. Karay cites several testimonies about SS officer Fritz Bartenschlager, who attended selections in order to choose "escort girls."[79] In October 1942, five Jewish women were taken to a party at his apartment, where they were forced to serve the guests in the nude, and were ultimately raped by these same guests.[80] A few months later, at a similar party in January 1943, which included the attendance of the SS commander of Radom, three Jewish women renowned throughout the camp for their extraordinary beauty, were brutally raped.[81] It is fair to conclude that because these women were young and beautiful, and forced to walk around naked, sexual violence was primarily motivated by the men's desire to be sexually aroused and fulfilled by the women's attractive female bodies.

The venereal appetites of German men are also apparent in the testimony of Gertrude Schneider of the Belorussian ghetto. Schneider testifies that the German Commander, SS Officer Krauser, was a sexual deviant, who "loved young, pretty girls. He did. When he liked you, that was it, you got a better

---

[79]   Felicia Karay, *Death Comes in Yellow: Skarzysko-Kamienna Slave Labor Camp* (Amsterdam: Overseas Publishers Association, 1996), 80.

[80]   Felicia Karay, "Women in the Forced Labor Camps," in *Women and the Holocaust,* 290-291.

[81]   Ibid.

Kommando . . . He had one girl friend. She was Olly Adler and she was breathtakingly beautiful. I don't care what beauties you see here, she was so striking that when she walked into the ghetto and he saw her, he actually fell apart right on the spot"[82] and Krauser kept this "breathtakingly beautiful" Jewish woman as his sexual slave. Both the specific reference to Adler's beauty and the claim that Krauser "fell apart of the spot" when he first saw Adler indicate that sexual fulfillment was the primary motivating factor in the rape of Olly Adler.

And so it went from region to region.[83] The occurrences of rape are extensive, making it clear that Jewish women were vulnerable to the sexual desires of German men wherever they were situated within Nazi occupied Europe. The pattern that emerges from much of the evidence supports the notion that many perpetrators were motivated to rape by a desire for sexual activity. It is important to note that a majority of the testimonies mention the beauty of the victim, highlighting that these women were selected in large part for their attractiveness, or at least this was the perception of the

---

[82] Esther Katz and Joan Ringelheim, ed. *Proceedings of the Conference on Women Surviving the Holocaust* (New York: Institute for Research in History, 1983), 48.

[83] Further testimonies that report German men raping Jewish women throughout Nazi Occupied Europe, are those of Laura Hillman of the Lublin Ghetto in Poland, Interview Code 1208, USC Shoah Foundation Testimony; Sara Dickerman, survivor of the Ppeatow Ghetto, Interview Code 26007, USC Shoah Foundation Testimony; Shari Braun of Augsburg Concentration Camp, Interview Code 1249, USC Shoah Foundation Testimony; Yolan Frank, survivor of Auschwitz II-Birkenau Concentration Camp, Interview Code 35354, USC Shoah Foundation Testimony; Zuzana Adam of Miskolc Ghetto in Hungary, Interview Code 14708, USC Shoah Foundation Testimony.

observer. The perpetrators' selection of beautiful women, at the ages of peak physical attractiveness, reinforces what psychologists refer to as the biosocial rape theory, which argues that wartime rape is largely motivated by sexual desire.[84] Research demonstrates that, across societies, young women are considered the most desirable, and therefore young and attractive women will be overrepresented as the victims of wartime rape.[85] In the context of the Holocaust, the anecdotal accounts leave little doubt to the theory's accuracy, as attractive Jewish women were often selected as the sexual outlets for the perpetrators carnal desires.

It is clear that German men throughout the Eastern occupied territories raped Jewish women. These men were willing to break racial laws to fulfill their sexual needs and the German leadership's lenient stance regarding such offenses provided the perpetrators with a tacit blessing to rape.[86] Although rape was

---

[84] The biosocial theory is most often identified with the work of biologist Randy Thornhill and anthropologist Craig Palmer. See, Randy Thornhill and Craig Palmer, *A Natural History of Rape* (Massachusetts: The MIT Press, 2000).

[85] Jonathan, Gottschall, "Explaining Wartime Rape." *The Journal of Sex Research,* Vol. 41, No. 2 (May 2004): 134.

[86] According to Birgit Beck, some judges treated German rapists with pity because of the difficult situation on the eastern front. They declared that the lack of sexual intercourse and the large amounts of alcohol consumed should be considered "extenuating circumstances" and should not be punished severely, especially if it was the perpetrator's first offense. This so-called 'sexual predicament' of soldiers was seriously taken into account when a sentence was given. See, Beck, "Rape: The Military Trials of Sexual Crimes Committed by Soldiers in the Wehrmacht, 1939-1944," in *Home Front: The Military, War, and Gender in the Twentieth Century Germany,* 265.

not a state sanctioned strategy of war, the perpetrators believed it was their right to rape Jewish women, a belief linked to their overall sexist attitude towards women, antisemitic ideological beliefs and conviction in their own racial superiority. Moreover, sexual pleasure through intercourse, whether coerced or not, could function as a coping mechanism for men. Physical intimacy helped to restore a sense of normalcy and emotional stability to perpetrators who were shaken by the job of killing.[87] Thus, in cases where sexual violence was largely motivated by a desire for sexual activity, it could simultaneously function as a means of enabling men to continue fulfilling their murderous tasks.

Brothels

Institutionalized sex was yet another form of sexual violence, wherein the perpetrators were largely motivated by a desire for sexual pleasure. In the Third Reich, a system of brothels was implemented for the use of both Nazi men and concentration camp prisoners. The existence of such brothels exemplifies how integral sexual satisfaction was to the Nazi enterprise of destruction. Sexual violence was extensive within the confines of the brothel walls, manifesting itself in the form of sexual slavery. German authorities, officers, and members of the SS, as well as non-Jewish prisoners frequented these brothels, and women of all different backgrounds, including Jewish women, were forced to work

---

[87] Doris Bergen, "Sexual Violence in the Holocaust: Unique and Typical?" in *Lessons and Legacies VII: The Holocaust in International Perspectives.* ed., Dagmar Herzog and Peter Hayes. (Norwest University Press, 2006), 187.

as prostitutes. The men who visited these brothels were largely motivated by a desire for sexual pleasure, an assertion which is supported by the brothels' reportedly long lines and high levels of attendance.[88] Although some cases of sexual violence within the brothels indicate motivations beyond sexual satisfaction, such as a desire to humiliate or to exert power, it seems that the primary motivation for attendees was the desire for sexual activity.

It is estimated by scholars that over 500 military brothels were established throughout the Third Reich during the course of World War II.[89] The German military leadership was largely concerned with providing their men with a sexual outlet, believing that satisfying soldiers' desires would be beneficial to the war effort.[90] Nazi authorities were evidently more concerned with ensuring the brothels were fully staffed with attractive women, than abiding by racial laws, as Jewish women and other "inferior" women were sometimes selected for this kind of sexual slavery. According to historian Christa Paul, a pioneer in the field of Nazi prostitution practices: "No doubt remains, that despite the prohibition on intercourse with Jews, Jewish women were taken away to military

---

[88] Survivors Arnold Lustig of Auschwitz, Heinz Heger of Flossenburg, and Eugen Kogon of Buchenwald report regularly long lines at the camp brothels. See, Arnold Lustig, *Lovely Green Eyes* (New York: Arcade Publishing, 2002); Heinz Heger, *The Men with the Pink Triangle.* trans. David Fernbach (London: Gay Men's Press, 1980); Eugen Kogon, *Theory and Practice of Hell* (New York: Octagon Books, 1973).

[89] Wendy Jo Gertjejanssen, "Victims, Heroes, Survivors," unpublished PhD. Dissertation (Minnesota: University of Minnesota, 2004), 223.

[90] Annette Timm, "Sex with a Purpose: Prostitution, Venereal Disease and Militarized Masculinity in the Third Reich," *Journal of the History of Sexuality,* 11, 2002, pp. 223-255.

brothels . . ."[91]Along similar lines, historian Robert Sommer contends that the "race" of the women selected for SS brothels was relatively unimportant. Instead, the most important factor was that the women selected were sexually appealing.[92] Sommer's argument is supported by an account of a Jewish survivor, who had been imprisoned in a brothel for the use by SS guards. The survivor recounts that during the first selection at Auschwitz, attractive Jewish women were "ordered out of the line" and "used for the most licentious purposes, kept alive solely to satisfy the base instincts of several sadistic and bestial Nazis."[93] Her testimony in confluence with the assertions made by Sommer and Paul, reveal that contrary to popular belief, Jewish women were indeed used in the SS brothels. Moreover, sexual satisfaction was of critical importance to the institutionalized system of sexual slavery. The German perpetrators were motivated to rape brothel inmates in large part because they wanted to engage in sexual intercourse with women whom they found sexually attractive and could therefore achieve maximal pleasure with. And most importantly, this pleasurable sexual activity could function as a release for the tensions produced by war.

The Nazis established brothels not only for the pleasure of German men, but also for the pleasure of productive prisoners. In June 1941, Himmler, while conducting an inspection of the

91   Catherine MacKinnon, *Are Women Human?: And Other International Dialogues* (Cambridge: Harvard University Press, 2006), 216.
92   Robert Sommer, "Camp Brothels: Forced Sex Labour in Nazi Concentration Camps," in *Brutality and Desire,* 169.
93   As quoted in, Catherine MacKinnon, *Are Women Human?: And Other International Dialogues*, 218.

Mauthausen concentration camp, made the decision to install a system of prisoner brothels within various concentration camps. By the summer of 1942, the construction of the prisoner brothels was well underway. Brothels were opened in ten of the major concentration camps.[94] Like the SS brothels, racial purity laws did not prevent the use of Jewish women in camp brothels. Multiple survivor testimonies indicate that racial laws were frequently broken, and Jewish women were selected despite their racial origin.[95] In his diary, survivor Heinz Heger supports this assertion and he reports that in general, most of the women at the Flossenburg brothel were of Jewish origin.[96] The fact that, on the whole, Nazi leadership turned a blind eye to these racial transgressions supports the assertion made by Elizabeth Heinemann that the supposed importance of fulfilling men's sexual drives surpassed the 'ethnic aim' of 'racial pureness.'[97]

The camp brothel was established for various reasons. Himmler, believing that satisfying male sexual desires improved military performance, decided that granting prisoners the right to

---

[94] The brothels were instituted in Mauthausen, Gusen, Flossenburg, Buchenwald, Auschwitz-Stammlager, Auschwitz-Monowitz, Neuengamme, Dachau, Sachsenhausen, and Mittelbau-Dora.

[95] See, Muhlhauser, "Between 'Racial Awareness' and Fantasies of Potency: Nazi Sexual Politics in the Occupied Territories of the Soviet Union, 1942-1945," in *Brutality and Desire War and Sexuality in Europe's Twentieth Century,* 207; Beck, "Rape: The Military Trials of Sexual Crimes Committed by Soldiers in the Wehrmacht, 1939-1944," in *Home Front: The Military, War, and Gender in the Twentieth Century Germany,* 267.

[96] Heinz Heger, *The Men with the Pink Triangle,* 99.

[97] Heinemann, "Sexuality and Nazism: The Doubly Unspeakable?" in, *Journal of the History of Sexuality,* 54.

frequent a brothel would have similar benefits, namely increased levels of production.[98] The Bonus Order System was thus created. The SS granted special privileges to hard-working prisoners, including the opportunity to visit the brothel.[99] The creation of the Bonus Order System is telling in that it highlights the high value the Nazis placed on sexual intercourse. In addition to increasing production efficiency, and satisfying the sexual desires of prisoners, SS men also frequented the camp brothels. Many made visits in the late hours of the night, thereby utilizing them for their own sexual pleasure as well.[100]

Henia Bryer, of the Majdanek concentration camp, reports that Jewish girls were indeed selected for work in the brothels. Bryer testifies that once the transports from the Lodz ghetto arrived at the Majdanek camp, the Germans: "selected over 100 young women. They were beautiful; each one of them was prettier than the other . . . Eventually we found out what happened to these girls . . . they were used for the German brothels."[101] Jewish women were also frequently selected for brothels from the women's concentration camp in Ravensbruck.[102] The selection process is explained in Ravensbruck survivor Margarete Neumann's memoir, wherein she describes a commission of SS officers arriving from Mauthausen, to select their female victims. The men "inspected

---

[98] Muhlhauser, 198.

[99] Robert Sommer, "Camp Brothels: Forced Sex Labour in Nazi Concentration Camps," in *Brutality and Desire,* 170.

[100] Kogon, 128.

[101] Henia Bryer, Interview Code 5970, USC Shoah Foundation Testimony

[102] Rochelle G. Saidel, *The Jewish Women of Ravensbruck Concentration Camp* (Madison: University of Wisconsin Press, 2004), 214.

the human flesh available . . . Those with firm breasts, sounds limbs, and general physical attractions were selected for the brothel in Mauthausen."[103] Jewish survivor Johanna Krause, also an inmate of Ravensbruck, provides a similar testimony: "They only took the good-looking women. The young Jewish women were particular favourites . . . I never saw any of these women again."[104] Once these women arrived at the brothels, they were examined for sexually transmitted diseases, and some were then sexually "tested," which meant raped by SS men.[105] In the evenings, once the male prisoners had finished their daily work, the women were forced to endure hours of sex. Women had to accept roughly ten men per evening, however reports vary, and in the Sachsenhausen brothel some women were forced to cater to over 40 men per day.[106]

There are various reasons why men chose to visit the camp brothel, however, based on multiple survivor testimonies and secondary research, the desire to satisfy sexual urges, and reaffirm potency, were among the most prevalent reasons offered. Buchenwald survivor and psychologist, Ernst Federn, claims, "sexuality played a tremendous role"[107] in the camps,

---

[103] Margarete Buber-Neumann, *Under Two Dictators,* trans. Edward Fitzgerald (London: V Gollancz, 1949), 199.

[104] Johanna Krause, *Twice Persecuted: Surviving in Nazi Germany and Communist East Germany.* ed., Carolyn Gammon and Christiane Hemker (Waterloo: Wilfrid Laurier Press, 2007), 75.

[105] Brigitte Halbmayr, "Women in Prisoner Brothels in Nazi Germany," in *Crimes Against Women* ed., David Pike (New York: Nova Science Publishers, Inc., 2011), 111.

[106] Halbmayr, 114.

[107] Sommer, 181.

and according to survivors Bruno Bettelheim and Eugen Kogon, virtually every man feared becoming impotent, thus the brothel offered a way to verify one's potency.[108] Survivor Heinz Heger also emphasizes the importance of sex to male inmates. In his memoir, *The Men with the Pink Triangle,* Heger reports that on the opening day of the Flossenburg brothel, around one-hundred men lined up to attend: "These prisoners . . . a good number of them half-starved and exhausted human wrecks, floating between life and death, and looking as if they might collapse at any minute. Yet they still wanted to have their 'pleasure'—a clear sign of how sexuality is the most powerful of human drives."[109] For the prisoners, the brothel therefore functioned to "reward" their labor and fulfill their sexual desires, while simultaneously functioning as an institution that both humiliated them and dehumanized their female victims. This system of sexual slavery evidently entailed a dual system of exploitation and as Elizabeth Heinemann has pointed out, "understanding this type of prostitution as an exchange between men and the state is a profound insight into the "rationalized" uses of sexuality-and its costs to women" during the Third Reich.[110]

From the body of evidence presented, it becomes clear that sex was of instrumental importance to both the Nazi regime and its perpetrators. The sexual abuse of Jewish women in brothels was largely motivated by a desire, on the part of the perpetrator, to have sex. And this form of coerced sexual intercourse functioned

---

[108] See, Bettelheim, *The Informed Heart,* 195-196; Eugen Kogon, *Theory and Practice of Hell,* 128.

[109] Heinz Heger, *The Men with the Pink Triangle*, 97.

[110] Elizabeth Heinemann, "Sexuality and Nazism: The Doubly Unspeakable?" in *Journal of the History of Sexuality* 11, (2002), 54.

as a means for men to achieve sexual pleasure. The laws against *Rassenschande* were clearly insufficient to deter such sexual abuses from occurring and the desire for sex drove men to not only rape Jewish women in brothels but in a diversity of contexts throughout Nazi-Occupied Europe. Sexual violence became an integral aspect of the Nazi machinery destruction wherein sexual slavery, and rape functioned as a means for the perpetrator to satisfy their male sexual urges. Moreover, the brothel provided German men with an opportunity to remove themselves from the horrors of war and find both comfort and sexual satisfaction with attractive women. Jewish women in the brothels thus became the sexual outlets for perpetrators to release tensions produced by the job of killing and war, which in turn, enabled many of them to more easily continue fulfilling their genocidal tasks.

CHAPTER 2
SEXUAL VIOLENCE AS MASCULINE EGO GRATIFICATION

Sexual violence also functioned as a form of masculine ego-gratification, which enhanced perpetrators' feelings of power, and camaraderie within their group. The male ego, explains anthropologist Peggy Sanday, is built upon sexual conquests, because "through sex men gain respect from other men" and affirm their masculinity.[111] Many of the men who acquired notoriety during the Holocaust for their sexual sadism and brutality, were individuals who before the Nazi regime were relatively unsuccessful in civilian life.[112] The new regime gave these men the opportunity to advance their career, and thereby enhance their masculine self-esteem. Perpetrating sexual violence can intensify men's already increased bravado associated with attaining a position of power, which is then further enhanced when the violence is validated by one's peers. Engaging in sexual violence thus offered the Nazi perpetrators the opportunity to not only gain acceptance and enhance their status within their social group, but to gratify their masculine ego.[113] Moreover, because sexual violence was perpetrated and even encouraged among some of the German guards and soldiers, as appears to have been the

---

[111] Peggy Sanday, *Fraternity Gang Rape* (New York and London: New York University, 2007), 92.

[112] Fogelman, "Rape During the Nazi Holocaust," in *Rape as a Weapon of War and Genocide,* 23.

[113] Fogelman, 23.

case in the following examples, it created a possibility to rape for opportunists who would not otherwise have raped because of social and/or legal sanctions.[114]

Eastern Occupied Territories

Instances of sexual violence motivated by these factors often entailed the sexual humiliation of a victim, gang or mass rape. For example, in different contexts throughout Nazi-Occupied Europe, members of the Wehrmacht, the SS, and the police, conducted body searches of Jewish women. These bodily searches were indeed sanctioned by Nazi regulations; however, instructions did not include the acts that many German men performed. Various testimonies describe the ways in which the perpetrators touched the victims' breasts, squeezed their nipples, spanked their buttocks, and invaded bodily orifices, as a means of entertaining one another. According to Jewish survivor Rachel Drabkin, during body searches the Germans took great pleasure in sexually humiliating Jewish women, stripping them naked, whipping their genitals and breasts with sticks, and laughing.[115] Warsaw ghetto diarist Mary Berg attests to similar instances of sexual humiliation. On January 10, 1941, Berg reported the following in her diary: "Last night we went through several hours of mortal terror. At about 11:00pm a group of Nazi gendarmes broke into the room where our house

---

[114]   Anette Houge, "Wartime Rape and Sexual Violence: A qualitative analysis of perpetrators of sexual violence during the war in Bosnia and Herzegovina," (Norway: University of Oslo, 2008), 50.

[115]   Rachel Drabkin, Interview Code 18294, USC Shoah Foundation Testimony

committee was holding a meeting. The Nazis ordered the women to strip hoping to find concealed diamonds. The women were kept naked for more than two hours while the Nazis put their revolvers to their breasts and private parts," and as Berg notes, "appeared thoroughly amused."[116] The fact that Berg mentions being kept naked with revolvers forced against her genitals indicates that, for her, there was a strong sexual element to this event.

Testimonies that discuss similar instances of sexual violations are numerous, and reveal that the Germans interpreted their regulations according to their own, often perverse, interests.[117] Perpetrating sexual violence, explains psychologist Eva Fogelman, adds to the already increased feelings of authority associated with being a Nazi, "having power and privileges, and the positive self-image gained from aggressive ideals."[118] The ego gratification of sexual violence is further heightened when validated by one's

---

[116] Mary Berg. *Warsaw Ghetto: Diary of Mary Berg.* (New York: L.B. Fischer Publishing Corp, 1945), 46.

[117] Among the memoirs and oral testimonies that discuss bodily searches by German men, all survivors testify to either experiencing the molestation of their breasts and genitals, or enduring sexually humiliating comments. For example, see Cecile Klein, *Sentenced To Live* (New York: Holocaust Library 1988) 73, 77. Klein describes the degrading body search she endured, testifying she was forced to strip naked, and then ordered to lie on her side on a wooden table. The SS officers gawked and jeered, and with a stick poked around her private parts. See also, Gizel Berman, Interview Code 6845, USC Shoah Foundation Testimony. Berman describes the humiliating and sadistic manner in which the Nazis conducted bodily searches, and testifies that men inserted their fingers in her vagina, and played with her breasts.

[118] Fogelman, "Rape During the Nazi Holocaust," in *Rape: Weapon of War and Genocide,* 23.

peers. When perpetrators share in sexual violence—as historian Dagmar Herzog puts it-they reaffirm their bonds with one another, thereby strengthening group camaraderie.[119] Moreover, sexual violence, particularly in the form of sexual humiliation, was for the perpetrators a means to compete with and entertain each other, which also enhanced feelings of masculinity and collective power.

Ghettos

The desire for masculine ego gratification and power also manifested itself in cases of gang rape. In the Warsaw ghetto, Jewish survivor Lusia Haberfeld testifies to instances of gang rape. German authorities entered Jewish homes demanding gold and valuables. During these home invasions, states Haberfeld, the Germans would routinely beat the Jewish occupants, followed by gang raping the Jewish women.[120] Similarly, the *Free Europe* pamphlet, *The Persecution of the Jews,* testifies: "As a result of a raid carried out in Francizskanska Street, 40 Jewish girls were dragged into the house which was occupied by the German officers. There, after being forced to drink, the girls were ordered to undress and to dance for the amusement of their tormentors. Beaten, abused, and gang raped, the girls were not released til 3:00am."[121] By collectively raping the Jewish girls, the responsibility for the

---

[119] Herzog, "Sexual Violence against Men," in *Rape: Weapon of War and Genocide,* 38.

[120] Lusia Haberfeld, Interview code 20848, USC Shoah Foundation Testimony

[121] Jacob Apenszlak, ed. *The Black Book of Polish Jewry: An Account of Martyrdom of Polish Jewry,* 29.

act of sexual violence was divided amongst the perpetrators. This diffusion of responsibility enabled the men to not only sustain their involvement in the violence, but allowed them to engage in more sadistic behaviour than they would alone.[122]

Concentration Camps

Within the concentration camp system, Jewish women also experienced gang rape at the hands of the Germans. A telling example is described by Jewish survivor, Erica Betts, who was incarcerated at the Dachau concentration camp and experienced gang rape. Betts testifies that German guards repeatedly raped her: "There was sex from morning to night and there was not anything you could do about it. Two or three would come in and you had to lie on the floor and that was it."[123] And at the Stutthof Concentration Camp, Germans also gang raped Jewish girls. Juliana Carpentieri tells of the sadistic gang rape she experienced in the soldiers barracks at the camp: "I was only a kid. They sodomized me, they raped me and then they said they were going to kill me. There were five of them. I cried out. All five of them raped me, laughing, drinking."[124] The fact that the perpetrators were laughing indicates that they found the rape 'entertaining' and 'enjoyable,' and as Anette Houge has noted in her examination of wartime rape, gang rape is often intended to bolster the masculine

---

[122]   James E. Waller, "Rape as a Tool of "Othering" in Genocide," in *Rape: Weapon of War and Genocide,* 94.

[123]   Erica Betts, Interview Code 20825, USC Shoah Foundation Testimony

[124]   Juliana Carpentieri, Interview Code 48403, USC Shoah Foundation Testimony

self-identity of all the men involved in the assault.[125] Moreover, gang rapes serve the function of reinforcing the group identity of the perpetrators, and thereby also increase loyalty among the men in the group.

It is clear from the various testimonies that the Germans seized sexual violence as a powerful tool of destruction. On the one hand, sex served as a means of enhancing the perpetrators' masculine ego and asserting their total power. At the same time however, acts of sexual violence, especially gang rape, opened a door to fraternization, and strengthened camaraderie. The interplay of such functions is aptly revealed through the testimony of Jewish survivor Lucyna Berkowicz. In Chruslice Poland, Lucyna was sexually assaulted, and testifies: "It was New Year's Eve. I was sitting in a room with a bunch of young girls . . . There came in a bunch of drunk Polish collaborators and Germans and they took out five or six women," including Lucyna, and subsequently took turns raping the women.[126] The sexual abuse of Jewish girls also occurred in the Ravensbruck concentration camp, where, as a child, Jewish survivor Sara M, was gang raped by German men. She recalls that a woman took her from her barracks, gave her candy, and left her in a small room: "There were two men there and there were some other people in the room, I think. I was put on a table. From what I remember, [it was] a table or it could have been

---

[125] Anette Houge, "Wartime Rape and Sexual Violence: A qualitative analysis of perpetrators of sexual violence during the war in Bosnia and Herzegovina," Unpublished PhD Dissertation, (Norway: University of Oslo, 2008), 48.

[126] Lucyna Berkowicz, Interview Code 22640, USC Shoah Foundation Institute Testimony.

a high table. I was very little so it seemed like it was very high up from where I was, and I was very violently sexually abused. And I remember being hit, I remember crying and I wanted to get out of there. And I was calling people and screaming and I remember one thing that stands out in my mind, that one of them told me that they would stand me up on my head and cut me right in half."[127]

In cases of gang rape, where the perpetrators take turns abusing, torturing and raping the victim, their primary motivation is not the satisfaction of sexual urges, rather masculine ego gratification and a means of reaffirming their power.[128] In these examples of gang rape it is important to note that the beauty of the victim is never mentioned, which is one indicator that sexual pleasure was not the primary motivator. Moreover, gang rapes are more aggressive than individual acts of rape motivated by sexual desire, and during gang rape the group, "puts pressure on the man to imitate his peers and live up to or even exceed their expectations with his actions."[129] Thus, for the individual perpetrator, gang rape functions as a means to demonstrate their masculine power and to prove their racial superiority before their peers. Furthermore, in the context of war and genocide, where men have power over the life and death of their victims, they often still find themselves vulnerable, and in a constant state of uncertainty. This combination facilitates

---

[127] Sara M, Interview Code 29016, USC Shoah Foundation Institute Testimony
[128] Eva Fogelman, "Rape During the Nazi Holocaust: Vulnerabilities and Motivations" in *Rape: Weapon of War and Genocide*, 19.
[129] Euan Hague, "Rape, Power and Masculinity: The Construction of Gender and National Identities in the War in Bosnia-Herzegovina," in *Gender and Catastrophe,* ed., Ronit Lentin (London & New York: Zed Books, 1997), 57.

sexual violence.[130] These polarized feelings of vulnerability and omnipotent power experienced by perpetrators, is explained by psychohistorian Robert J. Lifton. Sexual violence is often a sadistically motivated behaviour, and perpetrating such violence, argues Lifton, "is an aspect of omnipotence, an effort to eradicate one's own vulnerability and susceptibility to pain and death."[131] Therefore, sexual violence, which humiliates, degrades, and renders a victim completely powerless, functions as a means for perpetrators to increase feelings of omnipotent power, and enhance their masculine self-esteem and status within their social group.

Sexual violence, particularly gang rapes, should therefore be understood as an integral aspect of the Nazi machinery of destruction. By increasing the perpetrators' sense of camaraderie, power, and omnipotence, gang rape enabled individuals to engage in more sadistic behaviour than they would engage in alone. As Joshua Goldstein argues, gang rape seems to strengthen the allegiance and loyalty among men in small units. Most importantly, the feelings of ego-gratification, in confluence with collective delinquency, cause the individual perpetrator to lack any sense of remorse or responsibility.[132] Thus, sexual violence, by reaffirming men's masculinity, and confirming the bonds between them, ultimately strengthened the perpetrators' willingness to destroy, which became a critical component to the continued functioning of genocide.

---

[130] Dagmar Herzog, "Sexual Violence against Men: Torture at Flossenburg," in *Rape: Weapon of War and Genocide,* 38.

[131] Robert J. Lifton, *The Nazi Doctors: Medical Killing and the Psychology of Genocide* (New York: Basic Books, 1986), 447.

[132] Joshua Goldstein, *War and Gender. How Gender Shapes the War System and Vice Versa* (Cambridge: Cambridge University Press, 2001), 365.

CHAPTER 3
SEXUAL VIOLENCE AS A TOOL OF HUMILIATION

The Nazis seized sexual violence as a powerful tool of humiliation. Although many instances of sexual violence were motivated by a desire for sexual pleasure, or enhanced feelings of power and masculinity, the motivation to inflict humiliation by sexual means figures prominently in much of the evidence. For the perpetrators, whether intuitive or deliberate, humiliating their victims could function as a disengagement practice, which made their reprehensible conduct more acceptable. By humiliating Jewish women through acts of sexual violence, the perpetrators could more easily categorize them as subhuman, thus distancing themselves from the moral implications of their deadly actions. Instances of sexual violence that were primarily motivated by the desire to humiliate often entailed coerced nakedness, voyeurism, and the interference with genitalia. Such violations occurred in a diversity of contexts including the Eastern occupied territories, ghettos, and camps, however, as this section will demonstrate, the humiliation of Jewish woman was of particular importance within the concentration camp system.

Eastern Occupied Territories

In the first months after the German invasion of the Soviet Union, sexual violence was routinely seized as means to humiliate victims, as the Germans searched homes and interrogated the local people. Jewish women, and sometimes men, were forced to strip naked during these home invasions, and in some cases women were forced to perform menial tasks in the nude for the enjoyment of the perpetrators.[133] Regina Muhlhauser's study of sexual violence in the East reports such occurrences, revealing that Jewish women were forced to undress, bend down and pretend to clean the stairs of their house, while the German perpetrators watched.[134] Instances like this highlight the ways in which the perpetrators used sexual violence as a means to not only humiliate and degrade Jewish women, but also to entertain themselves and fulfill their perverse sexual fantasies.

Similar cases of inflicted humiliation are evident in the testimony of a Polish doctor in Warsaw who testified that the Germans regularly raped Jewish girls: "The Germans suddenly enter a house and rape 15-or 16-year old girls in the presence of their parents and relatives." This rape, committed in front of family members, was more than a localized sexual act; it functioned as a means to humiliate and degrade the entire family forced to watch helplessly. Similarly, in Minsk, on August 8 1941, German soldiers forcibly entered a Jewish home where they found a mother and her three children. The Germans grabbed the Jewish woman, and in front of her crying children, raped her "right there in the yard."[135]

---

[133] See for instance, Faye Schulman, *A Partisan's Memoir. Women of the Holocaust* (Toronto: Second Story Press, 1995), 65.

[134] Muhlhauser, "The Unquestioned Crime: Sexual Violence by German Soldiers during the War of Annihilation in the Soviet Union, 1941-45," in *Rape in Wartime,* 37.

[135] Ilya Ehrenburg and Vasily Grossman, *The Complete Black Book of Russian Jewry,* 212.

This instance of rape was also clearly more than a sexual act. By raping the Jewish woman in the presence of her children, this act of sexual violence functioned as a means to inflict severe humiliation. According to Regina Muhlhauser, the publicity of these rapes demonstrates the multilayered communicative functions of sexual violence, which are aimed not only at the abused victim, but also those who witness the abuse.[136] The action communicates to the Jewish woman and her children that they are not only completely powerless, but they are not fully human. Jewish Historian, Na'ama Shik is correct in her analysis regarding sexual violence, where she concludes that to the German rapists, Jewish women ceased being 'human women' and "became a wide-open bodily site that possessed signs of sex but contained no humanity."[137]

Ghettos

Sexual violence also functioned as a tool of humiliation in the ghettos, where German authorities were reluctant to deprive themselves of any opportunity to perpetrate sexual abuses. For example, survivor Dr. Edith Kramer of the Lodz ghetto reports that before deportation to a factory in Poland, the selected women were required to bathe: 'This provided a good chance for the SS men to beat the naked girls with whips," which Kramer describes, as of one of the greatest defilements.[138] For these women, the removal

---

[136] Muhlhauser, 40.

[137] Shik, "Infinite Loneliness," in *Lessons and Legacies VIII: From Generation to Generation* 151.

[138] Robert Ritvo and Dianna Plotki, *Sisters in Sorrow: Voices of Care in the Holocaust*, (Texas: A & M University Press, 1998), 134.

of their clothing and invasion of their intimate space was an act of sexual violence that caused severe humiliation. Nudity in front of SS men with whom these women had no relationship was an abnormal and grotesque experience, especially because many of these Jewish women were religiously observant, augmenting the shame and humiliation.[139]

In the Kaunas ghetto, Jewish survivor Frieda Frome testifies to similar incidents of sexual violence, which were clearly motivated by a desire to inflict humiliation. The Germans, during their search for valuables, would force their way into ghetto homes and Jewish girls were made to "undress and pose in the nude for the Nazis' entertainment. One girl had all the hair clipped from one side of her head. The SD laughed long and loudly at the freakish appearance the terrified girl made," augmenting her mortification and shame.[140] Sexual violence in the form of forced nudity was evidently an effective means for the perpetrators to humiliate and degrade Jewish women in the most intimate way possible. These violations not only inflicted humiliation, but also according to many testimonies, robbed women of their sense of dignity, thereby making it easier for the perpetrators to psychologically

---

[139] Ni Aolain, "Sex based Violence and the Holocaust: A Reevaluation of Harms and Rights in International Law," *Yale Journal of Law and Feminism*, 12 (2002), 55.

[140] Frome, *Dare to Dream*, 42.

remove Jewish women from the universe of ethical obligation and humanity.[141]

Concentration Camps

In the context of the concentration camp, the humiliation of Jewish women was a crucial component to the process of annihilation. By degrading Jewish women through various forms of sexual humiliation, perpetrators could more easily overcome feelings of empathy and concern for such women, perceiving them as different and inferior, thereby devoid of human qualities.[142] Many female survivors describe the concentration camp induction as one of the most humiliating Holocaust experiences. Forced nudity was part of the entry process into the camps, and therefore a degrading experience that all women suffered.[143] In a variety of

---

[141]   See, Lillian Kremer, "Women's Holocaust Writing: Memory and Imagination," in *Experience and Expression: Women, the Nazis, and the Holocaust.* Kremer, who examined various female testimonies, contends that forced nudity in front of German men was one of the most psychologically traumatic experiences for women, which left many women completely humiliated and degraded.

[142]   Nicola Henry, Tony Ward, and Matt Hirshberg, "A Multifactorial Model of Wartime Rape." *Aggression and Violent Behaviour,* 9:5 (2004).

[143]   It is important to note that men experienced this process too, however, men typically write of their induction in terms of a loss of personal autonomy and dignity not a form of sexual humiliation. Also, men mainly undressed in front of other men, unlike women who were forced to undress in front of male guards. See, Lillian Kremer, "Women in the Holocaust: Representation of Gendered Suffering and Coping Strategies in American Fiction," in *Experience and Expression: Women, the Nazis, and the Holocaust,* 264.

memoirs and testimonies, the feelings of shame, and humiliation are evident as women explain how they were forced to strip naked in the presence of male SS guards and inmates. Ada Levi was sent to Auschwitz in October 1943, and tells of her humiliation standing in front of a herd of SS men: "We were led to a block where the SS men yelled, 'Strip!' We took off our coats and stood there looking helplessly at each other. Then again that scream: 'Strip!' Yes, to strip naked, totally naked in front of these animals . . ."[144]

More often than not, the German men would make fun of their naked bodies, sometimes playing with their nipples and touching their genitalia.[145] Auschwitz survivor Eva Schloss remembers the SS, "walked around the room and jeered at the sight of our naked bodies. It amused them to pinch the buttocks of the women who were young and pretty. When one of the men passed beside me and pinched my buttocks I felt really humiliated."[146] In her memoir, Gisela Perl echoes similar sentiments, and describes the sadistic excitement the SS guards exhibited as women passed through the sauna. She explains the first room in which she was brought was filled with young SS men whose "eyes shone with expectation, their ape-like movements betrayed an unhealthy, abnormal sexual excitement."[147] The leering stares, suggestive insults, forced nudity and invasive methods of physical examination are clear

[144] Ada Levi, Interview Code 02202, USC Shoah Foundation Testimony.

[145] Shik, "Sexual Abuse of Jewish Women in Auschwitz-Birkenau," in *Brutality and Desire: War and Sexuality in Europe's Twentieth Century,* 229.

[146] Eva Schloss, *Eva's Story: A Survivor's Tale* (New York: W.H. Allen & Company, 1988), 230.

[147] Gisella Perl, *I was a Doctor in Auschwitz* (New York: Arno Press, 1979), 43.

expressions of sexual violence, that should be understood as a means for the perpetrators to entertain themselves, and demonstrate their power, through the humiliation of their victims.

Auschwitz-Birkenau survivor Fania Fenelon also describes instances of sexual violence that resulted in the deepest feelings of humiliation: "A couple months previous [Tauber] had brought a thousand women out into the snow, lined them up, entirely naked, in the freezing air, then, moving along their ranks, lifted their breasts with the tip of his whip. Those whose breast sagged went to the left, those whose breasts remained firm went to the right and were spared a little longer . . ."[148] a scene that aptly demonstrates the ways in which humiliation, power and sexual violence were inextricably linked. Moreover, in this example, sexual humiliation is directly linked to survival, as women whose breasts sagged were sent to the gas chamber. The sexual humiliations experienced by Jewish women and the accompanying feelings of degradation, contributed not only to a climate of dehumanization amongst the prisoners, but also enabled the perpetrators to view their victims as objects devoid of humanity. Forced nudity, menacing sexual comments, sticks jabbed into breasts, and defloration with fingers, were all sexual violations largely motivated by a desire to humiliate Jewish women. Through these acts of sexual violence, perpetrators could destroy their victims' last remaining ties to humanity, which was an essential component to the genocidal process.

---

[148] Fania Fenelon, *Playing for Time*. (New York: Atheneum Publishers, 1977), 158.

CHAPTER 4
SEXUAL VIOLENCE AS A TOOL OF DEHUMANIZATION

As evinced by the various testimonies, rape and sexual violence were multi-functional for the Nazi perpetrators. However, as the war progressed, and the Nazis moved into full-scale genocide, sexual violence increasingly functioned as a tool of dehumanization, in such a way as to permit, or even rationalize, the atrocities being committed. When victims are dehumanized by a variety of means, in particular sexual violence, the moral restraints against killing or harming them, argues social psychologist Herbert Kelman, become significantly less effective.[149] Among the various forms of sexual violence that functioned as tools of dehumanization, mass rape and public rape were arguably the most effective. It is important to note, however, in the subsequent examples of sexual violence, the dehumanization of Jewish women often occurs in combination with their humiliation, as they both serve very similar functions. Dehumanization and humiliation function to demean, degrade, and destroy the dignity of victims, however, in the context of the Holocaust, the process of dehumanization can be understood as a more extreme tool of destruction wherein human beings were transformed into

---

[149] Herbert Kelman, and Lee Hamilton, *Crimes of Obedience. Toward a Social Psychology of Authority and Responsibility* (New Haven and New York: Yale University Press, 1989), 163.

"specimens of the human animal."[150] And although it remains unclear whether such acts of sexual violence were perpetrated with the primary intention of dehumanizing the victim, or whether the dehumanization resulted as a byproduct of such violence, what is clear is that sexual violence was an indispensable tool of destruction in the Nazis' sadistic arsenal of annihilation.

Eastern Occupied Territories

In the East, instances of mass rapes are extensive. Various reports, and testimonies discuss countless cases of rape and sexual violations, committed in front of family members, and entire communities, often followed by the murder of the victim. The *Einsatzgruppen* were particularly brutal, shooting pregnant Jewish women in the stomach, conducting invasive searches of sex organs and anuses for valuables, and raping Jewish women before shooting them and throwing them into burial pits.[151] In such episodes of sexual violence, where the perpetrators commit sexual abuses outside the bounds of direct orders, the motivation to dehumanize victims is evident. By dehumanizing Jewish women, perpetrators removed normal moral constraints against violence, which, as historian James Waller argues, enabled these

---

[150] Julie Kuhlken, "Weapon of Sadness: Economic and Ethical Dimensions of Rape as an Instrument of War," in *Rape: Weapon of War and Genocide,* 169.

[151] Richard Rhodes, *Masters of Death: The SS Einsatzgruppen and the Invention of the Holocaust,* (New York: Random House, 2002), 185-186.

men to "initiate, sustain, and cope with their evil."[152] Moreover, by publically raping and brutalizing Jewish women, the perpetrators not only violate the individual victim, but exert maximum psychological damage on the community as well. Thus, despite racial laws, German soldiers in the East exploited the sexual opportunities afforded to them by war, and sexual violence, whether deliberately or not, functioned as an effective means of dehumanizing Jewish women and their families.

Ghettos

In the context of the ghettos, where the Nazis already had complete power over their Jewish victims, sexual violence functioned as a redundant tool of terror largely motivated by a desire to further dehumanize Jewish women. Within the ghetto atmosphere of general violence, abuse, and omnipresent murder, sexual violence often manifested itself in the form of public rape, which functioned to not only dehumanize the raped victim but the entire Jewish community. As Regina Muhlhauser points out, the exposed female body during an act of public rape is intended by the perpetrator to be seen. It is the visible proof of the complete powerlessness of both the victim and the spectators.[153] A telling example is provided in the testimony of Jewish survivor Marek Edelman. In the Warsaw ghetto, Edelman testifies, German men raped a Jewish girl in the presence of other Jews: "They waited in line and then raped her. After the line finished, this girl . . . she

---

[152]   Waller, "Rape as a Tool of "Othering" in Genocide," 93.
[153]   Muhlhauser, 40.

was very pale, naked and bleeding, and she slouched down into a corner. The crowd saw everything, and nobody said a word. Nobody so much as moved, and the silence continued."[154] This episode of sexual violence, perpetrated in the sight of fellow Jews, communicated a dehumanizing message to both the victim and onlookers. As Christopher Browning has aptly noted, instances of public rape are both "an act of violent domination over the powerless victim," as well as a ritual of humiliation aimed at dehumanizing the entire Jewish population forced to stand by and watch helplessly.[155]

Concentration Camps

In concentration camps, rape likewise functioned as a tool of dehumanization. Survivor Ruth Elias of Auschwitz wrote of her experience: "Drunken SS men sometimes made unexpected appearances in our block . . . Young Jewish women would be pulled from their bunks, taken away somewhere and raped."[156] She explains that she was spared because she lived on the third tier of the bunks, and concluded, "I cannot describe the pitiable state of these poor women when they came back to the barracks."[157] Jewish

---

[154]   Hanna Krall, *Shielding the Flame: An Intimate Conversation with Dr. Marek Edelman, the Last Surviving Leader of the Warsaw Ghetto Uprising,* trans. Joanna Stasinska (New York: Henry Holt & Company, 1986), 44.

[155]   Christopher Browning, *Remembering Survival: Inside a Nazi Slave Labor Camp* (New York, 2010), 191.

[156]   Ruth Elias, *Triumph of Hope: From Theresienstadt and Auschwitz to Israel* (New York: John Wiley, 1998), 120.

[157]   Elias, 120.

survivor Zora Goldenberg also discusses the prevalence of rape stating that the Germans took young Jewish girls from the barracks and in front of everyone would rape them. Almost every night, "we heard crying and screaming and yelling. It was not safe to go to the toilet at night if you were a young girl. They would rape you . . . We had to do everything in the barracks."[158] By dehumanizing the young Jewish girls through the act of public rape, and forcing other prisoners to watch, their dehumanization was symbolically projected onto the entire Jewish community, as fellow Jews were forced to hear the girls' screams or even worse, witness the rape.

Survivor Emil G. reports similar episodes of public rape in Auschwitz-Birkenau, testifying to the occurrence of an exhibitionist rape. The Germans arranged a "show" in which they selected twenty Jewish women to rape in front of one of the labor groups. Emil added that the prisoners were supposed to stand and applaud.[159] These instances of rape clearly functioned as a means to dehumanize and humiliate the victims and the powerless bystanders. The fact that the other prisoners were made to stand and applaud is powerful evidence that this was intended as an act of dehumanization that also functioned to inflict severe humiliation on both the Jewish women and the labor group. Moreover, through such acts of sexual violence, the Nazis instilled a sense of terror throughout concentration camps; thereby keeping camp populations compliant and ensuring they remained utterly demeaned and degraded.

---

158 Zora Goldenberg, Interview Code 9471, USC Shoah Foundation Testimony.

159 Emil G. Interview Code 19178, USC Shoah Foundation Testimony.

Various testimonies also refer to the presence of dogs during episodes of rape, adding to the dehumanization of the victim.[160] In her memoir, *Five Chimneys,* Jewish survivor Olga Lengyel reports that a mother was forced to undress her daughter and then watch while trained Nazi dogs violated the girl.[161] Auschwitz-Birkenau survivor, Rachel Hanan, recounts the same event, corroborating Lengyel's testimony, adding that the girl died as a result of the brutal violation.[162] This was not an isolated incident but what is particularly important about this case is that it involved both a Jewish woman and child. The perpetrators seized sexual violence as a means of dehumanizing the victims, and destroying their dignity. By stripping the young girl naked, and forcing dogs to sexually violate her, the perpetrators created a situation wherein the victim was reduced to the status of an animal, no longer belonging to the realm of humanity. It is more than likely that the perpetrators found it necessary to dehumanize the woman and child in order to overcome their aversion to murdering innocent women and children. As historian Doris Bergen has argued, sexual violence is a particularly effective form of dehumanization, because, "sexual activities and sexual organs are so closely associated with

---

[160] For example, one survivor testifies: "that women were always tortured naked, to the deep enjoyment of the torturers. The SS men kept two German shepherd dogs. One was trained to lunge and bite. The other was trained to mount naked women who had first been ordered on their hands and knees . . ."see, J. Miller, *One by One by One: Facing the Holocaust* (New York: Simon & Schuster, 1990), 123 as cited in, Beverley Chambers, "Sexual Villainy in the Holocaust," PhD Dissertation Abstract (University of Ottawa, 2011), 6.

[161] Lengyel, *Five Chimneys,* 186.

[162] Rachel Hanan, Interview Code 13096, USC Shoah Foundation Testimony

individual and group honour," therefore by sexually violating a woman's body, her dignity and humanity are largely destroyed.[163]

Clearly, sexual violence functioned not only as an expression of hatred, sexual desire, power, and humiliation, but also served the practical function of dehumanization. Within the Nazi camp universe, perpetrators routinely seized sexual violence as a means to further dehumanize Jewish women, which arguably enabled them to psychologically distance themselves from their prey. Sociologist Zygmunt Bauman confirms this assertion, and argues that moral inhibitions against violence are undermined when victims are dehumanized.[164] Furthermore, sexual violence provided the perpetrators the opportunity to not only dehumanize the individual victims, but also the members of the Jewish community forced to witness the sexual atrocities. Moreover, Nazi ideology, as the evidence has demonstrated, did not constitute a barrier to sexual violence. Rather, ideology shaped the forms in which sexual violence was manifested, and the functions it served for the regime. Whether a direct or indirect consequence of sexual violence, dehumanization facilitated the destruction of Jewish women's claims to humanity, thereby enabling perpetrators to overcome "deeply internalized taboos against murdering innocent victims,"[165] which was essential to the continued functioning of genocide.

---

[163] Bergen, 188.

[164] Zygmunt Bauman, *Modernity and the Holocaust* (New York: Cornell University Press, 2000), 102.

[165] Heinemann, "Sexuality and Nazism: The Doubly Unspeakable," in *Sexuality and German Fascism,* 61.

SECTION III

THE CONNECTION BETWEEN SEXUAL VIOLENCE AND MURDER

By now, it is evident that Jewish women experienced sexual violence during the Holocaust and this violence thrived in both camp and non-camp settings throughout Nazi-Occupied Europe. Jewish women experienced this violence in many forms; however, from the large body of evidence examined a particular pattern involving rape emerges. Specifically, that the rape of Jewish women was frequently followed by their immediate murder; a pattern that should not go unnoticed. This section will attempt to complicate our view of rape during the Holocaust by demonstrating that a connection between rape and murder does indeed exist. Instances of rape followed by immediate murder were arguably a byproduct of three distinctive features of the Nazi regime: the laws against *Rassenschande,* the prohibition against Jewish women reproducing, and the implementation of the "Final Solution."

Rape Facilitating Murder

The Third Reich explicitly prohibited all sexual relations, whether consensual or not, between Aryans and Jews. To engage in such relations was considered the crime of *Rassenschande* (racial defilement). Although severe punishment for committing the crime was not always enforced, and the adjudication of *Rassenschande* cases was often erratic, it was still considered an especially heinous offense.[166] In spite of such laws, however, there were German men who raped Jewish women, and for these individuals, the laws against *Rassenschande* had little restraining effect. Yet, *Rassenschande* was important enough to the Nazi state that its violation, and potential reproductive consequences, made it necessary for perpetrators to immediately murder their Jewish victims. Therefore, perpetrators used the very same ideology, which prohibited sexual relations between Aryans and Jews in order to prevent racial degeneration, as the ideological justification to murder the Jewish women they raped.

The Nazi regime also fostered a preoccupation with regulating female sexuality, and prohibited Jewish women from reproducing through forced sterilization, abortion, and murder.[167] As historian Lawrence Langer has noted, the Nazis inverted birth into death, so that childbirth became a death warrant for the mother and

---

[166] Beck, "Rape: The Military Trials of Crimes Committed by soldiers in the Wehrmacht, 1939-1944," 266.

[167] Gisela Bock, "Racism and Sexism in Nazi Germany: Motherhood, Compulsory Sterilization, and the State," in *When Biology Became Destiny,* ed. Bridenthal et al., 271-296.

child.[168] Within this context, if a Jewish woman became pregnant
as a result of rape by an Aryan man, racial theory and Nazi law
left the perpetrator with only one practical solution: murder.
By killing their Jewish victim, the perpetrator ensured that all
evidence of their transgression was destroyed.[169] Therefore, Nazi
ideology, although so inconsistently applied that it could not
prevent cases of *Rassenschande,* was powerful enough to justify
the murder of a Jewish woman in order to prevent births. The Nazi
perpetrators allowed urges, such as the desire for sexual pleasure,
masculine ego gratification, and power, to overcome state-imposed
prohibitions against *Rassenschande,* and using the same ideology,
rationalized the murder of their Jewish rape victim as a necessary
racial health measure.

This precautionary measure was common practice among the
German rapists, especially within the Skarzysko-Kamienna Slave
Labor Camp. In her detailed study of the camp, Felicja Karay
reports that many of the German commanders would select the
most beautiful Jewish women of each newly arrived transport to
serve as personal sex slaves. The overwhelming majority of these
women were murdered once the men grew tired of them, however,
those women who became pregnant were murdered immediately
upon discovery of the pregnancy.[170] Milla Doktorczyk, a

---

[168] Lawrence Langer, "Gendered Suffering? Women In Holocaust
Testimonies," in *Women in the Holocaust,* 352-353.

[169] Doris Bergen, "Sex, Blood, and Vulnerability: Women Outsiders in
German-Occupied Europe," in *Social Outsiders in Nazi Germany*, ed.
Robert Gellately and Nathan Stoltzfus (Princeton and Oxford: Princeton
University Press, 2001), 277.

[170] Karay, *Death Comes in Yellow,* 95-96.

Skarzysko-Kamienna camp survivor, tells of her Jewish friend, Hochma, who was raped and then murdered by the Germans: "They raped her a couple of times . . . They took her away, into the office, took off her clothes . . . there were maybe four or five of them. One after another. Then they killed her and threw her out."[171] Another Jewish survivor of the camp recalls the German foreman of the camp, Krause, who would often get drunk, select a few Jewish women to rape, and "later they were shot so that there would be no "race pollution."[172] Similarly, on January 23, 1943, the German commander of Werk A, selected three Jewish girls, all acclaimed for their outstanding beauty, to serve German men at a dinner party. These women, testifies Karay, were all brutally raped and then subsequently slaughtered,[173] highlighting the inextricability of rape and death for many Jewish women during the Holocaust.

Incidences of rape and murder are also reported throughout the Eastern occupied territories. In Latvia, for example, in a small house on Mariinskaya Street, the Germans herded several dozen Jewish girls to their orgy, "forced them to strip naked, and dance and sing songs. Many of these unfortunate girls were raped right there and then taken out to the yard to be shot."[174] These episodes of murderous rape, taken in combination with

---

[171] Milla Doktorczyk, Interview Code 15012, USC Shoah Foundation Testimony

[172] Roma Tcharnobroda, Interview 24 September 1946, Munich, Germany, transcribed by David P. Boder, *Voices of the Holocaust: A Documentary Project by Illinois Institute of Technology*.

[173] Karay, *Death Comes in Yellow*, 81.

[174] Ehrenburg and Grossman, *The Complete Black Book of Russian Jewry*, 302.

the previous testimonies that report similar occurrences, support the conclusion that there is a persistent connection between the rape of Jewish women and murder. It is clear that many German perpetrators did not consider cases of rape that ended in murder as instances of *Rassenschande.* By immediately murdering their Jewish victims, the perpetrators erased the evidence of their racial transgression and its potentially incriminating racial consequences. It is therefore fair to assert, that as a result of National Socialism's racist guiding principles, which forbade the rape of Jewish women and their reproduction, German perpetrators had a strong incentive to destroy the evidence of their sexual crimes. Nazi racial policies thus created a seemingly contradictory situation, wherein the rape and impregnation of a Jewish woman was a violation of Nazi law, however, the murder of Jewish women was not considered a crime at all.

The Intersection of Rape and the "Final Solution"

The implementation of the "Final Solution" also fostered a connection between rape and murder. Before 1941, the groundless murder of Jews, although not considered a serious offense, was not a state-sanctioned policy nor fully legal. With the advent of the "Final Solution," however, the last remaining legal barriers against the murder of Jews were removed. As a result of this murderous policy's implementation, all Jews were slated for annihilation, which created a fertile ground for uninhibited acts of lethal rape to occur. For the German rapists, the fact that their potential victims would soon be murdered anyway, provided them with unprecedented sexual opportunity. This is made clear through

the testimony of Lilya Samoilovna Gleizer, who survived the
Minsk Pogrom in 1942. She reports: "the drunken Germans and
policeman raped young Jewish girls without a trace of shame . . .
They took their knives and cut out sex organs . . . cut off noses,
breasts, and ears."[175] Survivors of the Lvov ghetto report similar
occurrences during the ghetto's liquidation, testifying "the
unrestrained representatives of the 'master race' did not spare
a single Jewish woman during this 'campaign.' They raped and
murdered them."[176] Because these Jewish women were to be
murdered anyways, the perpetrators raped with impunity, and
without fear of consequence.

Survivor Joseph Tyl testifies to similar occurrences, and
reports that there was a certain SS guard: "He was a pervert who
killed for pleasure. He was also a sex maniac, who satisfied his
lust with young Jewish girls, who he murdered immediately
after he raped them."[177] Even on the way to the gas chambers,
Jewish women were viewed as sexually available. According to
survivor testimony, Treblinka guard Ivan Demaniuk, would stab
Jewish women's genitals and rape them before they entered the
gas chambers.[178] Erna Hilfstein, survivor of the Krakau-Plaszow
forced labor camp in Poland, provides a similar testimony, wherein

---

175 Ehrenburg and Grossman, *Complete Black Book of Russian Jewry,* 130
176 Ibid., 78
177 Eugene Aroneanu, *Inside the Concentration Camps: Eyewitness
     Accounts of Life in Hitler's Death Camps,* trans. Thomas Whissen
     (Westport: Praeger Publishers, 1996), 34.
178 Testimony of Eli Rozenberg, *Yad Vashem Archives*, as cited in, Beverley
     Chambers, "Sexual Villainy in the Holocaust," 7.

murder also facilitates the rape of a Jewish victim.[179] In 1943, Hilfstein explains, there was a work group of roughly forty Jews, thirty-nine men, and one woman. Upon their return from their workplace in Krakau, the camp commander immediately ordered the execution of the entire group. Every Jew was shot, however, the Jewish girl was shot in such a way that she did not immediately die. As a result, testifies Hilfstein, "they decided to rape her."[180] The fact that the victim was on the verge of death and had already been sentenced for execution provided the perpetrators with the sexual opportunity to rape without any fear that their actions would result in undesirable legal or reproductive consequences.

Rape and death also coalesced in the Lodz ghetto. In August of 1944, the leading German bureaucrat of the city, Hans Biebow, raped a young Jewish girl and then shot and murdered her.[181] According to testimonies of survivors from the Lodz ghetto, "Biebow practiced his sadistic whims . . . rapes of girls in the women's camp, savage outrages on captured Jews," which reveals that his sadistic behaviour was not unusual.[182] What is interesting about this episode of rape and murder is that it occurred in the final days of the Lodz ghetto's existence. The Jewish victim would have been sent to her death shortly after the rape took place, however, Biebow chose to murder her immediately, highlighting the fact

---

[179] Erna Hilfstein, Interview Code 9995, USC Shoah Foundation Testimony.

[180] Ibid.

[181] Isaiah Trunk, *Lodz Ghetto: A History,* ed., Robert Moses Shapiro (Bloomington: Indiana University Press, 2006), 266.

[182] Trunk, *Lodz Ghetto,* 269.

that genocidal conditions created a fertile ground for acts of rape followed by murder to occur.

Similarly, a survivor from the Warsaw ghetto recalls the rape and murder of Jewish girls, and reports that: "At night the Germans would force their way into Jewish homes and rape women and girls . . . Some of the girls, those of the more educated type, would be taken by the Germans to their barracks where they were raped and killed."[183] Likewise, in early September 1941, in a camp at Tulchin, Ukraine, the German camp commandant, "asked each night for two Jewish virgins," who he later killed.[184] And in the Auschwitz concentration camp, German soldiers, testifies survivor Annamarie Sokoly, raped multiple young Jewish girls. In the spring of 1944, Sokoly reports: "we heard their screams. We heard their cries. We heard the mothers cry. We never saw them again. They raped them. Whatever happened to them after, we never found out."[185] Because these young girls were destined for the gas chambers, their rape and murder presented perpetrators with little to no mental afflictions or fear of legal repercussions, creating unbridled sexual opportunity.

The "Final Solution," which slated all Jewish women for annihilation, can therefore be understood as a policy that facilitated an atmosphere conducive to murderous rape. Rape was not part of

---

[183] Jacob Apenszlak, *The Black Book of Polish Jewry,* 9.

[184] The Jewish Black Book Committee, *The Black Book: The Nazi Crime Against the Jewish People* (New York: Duel, Sloan and Pierce, 1946), 164.

[185] Testimony of Annamarie Sokoly, Interview Code 28195, USC Shoah Foundation Testimony.

the official genocidal plan but rather the consequence of favorable conditions and impunity. Within this context of omnipresent murder, the German perpetrators took unspeakable sexual liberties, exploiting the condemned fate of Jewish women, and utilizing it as a license to rape. Thus, during the Holocaust, rape not only facilitated the murder of Jewish women but also paradoxically was facilitated by murder.

CONCLUSION

By opening up our perspective-with a broad definition of
sexual violence, the use of survivor memoirs and testimonies, and
an understanding that Nazi racial laws were not religiously adhered
to nor followed-we find that the atrocities of the Holocaust had a
strong sexual component. And these atrocities took many forms,
occurred in a diversity of contexts, and served various functions for
the perpetrators. In most genocides, sexual violence is part of the
policy of the perpetrators, however, during the Holocaust, sexual
violence was not a state sanctioned policy; it was employed in a

haphazard manner that was horrific, multi-faceted, and deadly.[186] The genocidal conditions created an environment conducive to such violence by diminishing perpetrators' sensitivity to suffering, intensifying their sense of entitlement, and reinforcing notions of their racial superiority. And although laws against *Rassenschande* officially forbade sexual relations between Aryans and Jews, the rape of Jewish women still occurred. Nazi anti-Jewish practice and law varied significantly based on location and leadership, and as a result, what took place during the Holocaust did not always match the directed racial policy.[187] Moreover, far from protecting Jewish

---

[186] For example, during the war in Bosnia-Herzegovina, the rape of enemy women was a state-sanctioned policy. See. Alexandra Stiglmayer, "The Rapes in Bosnia-Herzegovina," in *Mass Rape: The War against Women in Bosnia-Herzegovina*, ed. Alexandra Stiglmayer (Lincoln and London: University of Nebraska Press, 1994); During the Rwanda genocide, women were raped on an even greater scale, as rape was seized as a weapon of war. See, Meredith Turshen, "The Political Economy of Rape: An Analysis of Systematic Rape and Sexual Abuse of Women during Armed Conflict in Africa," in *Victims, Perpetrators or Actors? Gender, Armed Conflict and Political Violence,* ed. Caroline Moser and Fiona C. Clark (London and New York: Zed Books, 2001). Rape-as-policy was also employed in the Ugandan war, between 1980 and 1986, and as a result 70 percent of women reported being raped by soldiers. See, Meredith Turshen, "The Political Economy of Violence against women during Armed Conflicts in Uganda." *Social Research,* 67, (2000). In Darfur, rape was a state-sanctioned policy, used as a weapon of destruction. See, Samuel Totten, "The Darfur Genocide: The Mass Rape of Black African Girls and Women", in *Plight and Fate of Women during and following Genocide,* ed. Samuel Totten (New Brunswick: Transaction Publishers, 2009).

[187] Helene J. Sinnreich, "The Rape of Jewish Women During the Holocaust," in *Sexual Violence Against Jewish Women During the Holocaust,* 109.

women from sexual violence, Nazi racial theory seems to have
only shaped the forms that sexual violence took, and influenced
how it functioned.

As I have argued, in the Nazi system of mass death, the
motivation to perpetrate sexual violence was clearly not uniform.
Perpetrators were motivated by a diversity of factors, including, a
desire for power, camaraderie, sexual pleasure and masculine ego-
gratification. Moreover, as the examination of various instances of
sexual violence has indicated, sexual violence was multi-functional
for the Nazi regime, operating as a powerful tool of humiliation
and dehumanization. As the Nazi regime moved into full-scale
genocide, sexual violence became an increasingly integral
component to the process of annihilation. By dehumanizing
Jewish women through varied forms of sexual violence, German
perpetrators increasingly saw their victims as less than human,
thereby further removing them from the realm of moral and ethical
obligation. Sexual violence was clearly an essential component to
the continued functioning of genocide, because through the process
of Jewish women's dehumanization, perpetrators were able to more
easily continue fulfilling their murderous tasks.

It is also my conclusion that rape and death were inseparably
intertwined for Jewish women, who, if raped by a German,
would likely be murdered afterwards. If a Jewish woman became
pregnant as a result of rape, in theory and in practice she had
to be murdered. This precautionary and murderous measure
was common practice among the German perpetrators who
wanted to destroy the evidence of their racial transgressions. The
implementation of the "Final Solution" likewise facilitated the

likelihood that incidents of rape would end in murder. The fact that Jewish women were ultimately slated for annihilation created a fertile ground for acts of rape followed by murder to occur. The Nazi perpetrators interpreted the regime's genocidal policy in terms that encouraged the performance of sexual violence, and utilized the "Final Solution" as an opportunity to rape with impunity.

This study has revealed that sexual violence against Jewish women during the Holocaust not only happened but it was extensive. It has also explored how sexual violence functioned and became part of the process of annihilation in the Third Reich. Instances of sexual violence ranged from gang rape and sexual slavery, to sexualized humiliation and genital mutilations, to inventive sadisms and murderous rape, all of which served different functions for its perpetrator.[188] Sometimes sexual violence was motivated by a desire to satisfy sexual urges, other times it was a way of demonstrating one's power. It was also seized as a means to reaffirm bonds among perpetrators, increase their feelings of power, and enhance their masculine ego. Sexual violence likewise functioned as an outlet for German men to release tensions produced by war that might have otherwise interfered with killing operations. But most importantly, it functioned as an effective tool of humiliation and dehumanization. What becomes clear is that during the Holocaust, sexual violence was multi-functional for the regime and its perpetrators, and became an integral component of the Nazi machinery of destruction.

---

[188] Herzog, *Brutality and Desire,* 4.

The Victims

The study of women and the Holocaust has undoubtedly become a significant and respected field within Holocaust studies. With its establishment and recent developments in the wider field of genocide studies, the topic of sexual violence against Jewish women during the Holocaust has begun to be uncovered. Many Holocaust scholars are beginning to acknowledge the importance of the study of sexual violence, recognizing it as a critical line of inquiry in need of greater investigation. For those historians unsure of the significance or legitimacy of the subject, they should be reminded that prioritizing the strictly murderous dimension of genocide above all else inhibits the full measure of victims' experiences from being understood. Furthermore, it severely diminishes the significance and severity of sexual violence, and its long-term effects.

For Jewish women, the consequences of sexual violence extended far beyond the Holocaust, as they were forced to carry forward the devastating aspects that their violations entailed. Many experienced physical traumas including internal injuries, venereal disease, and unwanted pregnancies, while almost all experienced psychological trauma, accompanied by feelings of shame and humiliation. On the whole, victims of sexual violence have felt obliged to stay silent about their experiences, fearing they did not fit within the traditional version of Holocaust narratives. Even worse, many found themselves ostracized by their communities, who labeled them as "loose," "whores by choice," and "immoral."[189] By complicating our view of women's Holocaust experiences through the recognition that sexual violence did occur, it allows the full measure of Jewish women's experiences under the Nazis to be told and can also promote the healing of the surviving victims.

Future Studies

Future studies of sexual violence during the Holocaust would benefit from approaching the subject in a systematic manner, examining every instance of sexual abuse in all its complex dimensions. By examining the forms of sexual violence, the context in which it occurs, the victim and the perpetrator, studies can achieve more nuanced understandings of the relationship between sexual violence and the genocidal process. More importantly, the multiple functions that sexual violence served and its implications for the functioning of the Nazi regime can be increasingly illuminated. Finally, the impact that sexual violence had on perpetrators must also be examined in order to understand the effect and consequences that perpetrating sexual violations entailed for the men who committed them. Thus, the study of sexual violence during the Holocaust has the potential to yield new and critical insights not only into the experiences of the victims but also into the ideological character of Nazism, and its perpetrators.

---

[189]   Levenkron, "Death and the Maidens," in *Sexual Violence Against Jewish Women during the Holocaust,* 24.

BIBLIOGRAPHY

Primary Sources:

Unpublished Oral Testimonies

University of Southern California Shoah Foundation Institute Visual History Archive (VHA)

Testimony of Zuzana Adam, *Yad Vashem Archives* (YVA) USC Shoah Foundation Institute, Interview 14708.

Testimony of Gizel Berman, *Yad Vashem Archives* (YVA) USC Shoah Foundation Institute, Interview 6845.

Testimony of Lucyna Berkowicz, *Yad Vashem Archives* (YVA) USC Shoah Foundation Institute, Interview 22640.

Testimony of Erica Betts. *Yad Vashem Archives* (YVA). USC Shoah Foundation Institute. Interview 20825.

Testimony of Irene Binzer. *Yad Vashem Archives* (YVA). USC Shoah Foundation Institute. Interview Number 28053.

Testimony of Sherri Braun, *Yad Vashem Archives* (YVA) USC Shoah Foundation Institute, Interview 1249.

Testimony of Henia Bryer. *Yad Vashem Archives* (YVA). USC Shoah Foundation Institute. Interview 5970.

Testimony of Juliana Carpentieri, *Yad Vashem Archives* (YVA). USC Shoah Foundation Institute. Interview 48403.

Testimony of Sara Dickerman. *Yad Vashem Archives* (YVA) USC Shoah Foundation Institute. Interview 26007.

Testimony of Milla Doktorczyk, *Yad Vashem Archives* (YVA). USC Shoah Foundation Institute. Interview 15012.

Testimony of Rachel Drabkin. *Yad Vashem Archives* (YVA). USC Shoah Foundation Institute. Interview 18294.

Testimony of Yolan Frank, *Yad Vashem Archives* (YVA) USC Shoah Foundation Institute. Interview 35354.

Testimony of Emil G. *Yad Vashem Archives* (YVA). USC Shoah Foundation Institute. Interview 19178.

Testimony of Zora Goldenberg. *Yad Vashem Archives* (YVA). USC Shoah Foundation Institute. Interview 9471.

Testimony of Lusia Haberfeld. *Yad Vashem Archives* (YVA). USC Shoah Foundation Institute. Interview 20848.

Testimony of Rachel Hanan. *Yad Vashem Archives* (YVA). USC Shoah Foundation Institute. Interview 13096.

Testimony of Erna Hilfstein, *Yad Vashem Archives* (YVA). USC Shoah Foundation Institute. Interview 9995.

Testimony of Laura Hillman. *Yad Vashem Archives* (YVA). USC Shoah Foundation Institute. Interview 1208.

Testimony of Ada Levi. *Yad Vashem Archives* (YVA). USC Shoah Foundation Institute. Interview 02202.

Testimony of Sara M, *Yad Vashem Archives* (YVA) USC Shoah Foundation Institute, Interview 29016.

Testimony of Annamarie Sokoly, *Yad Vashem Archives* (YVA) USC Shoah Foundation Institute, Interview 28195.

Illinois Institute of Technology Archives. David Boder Interviews (*Voices of the Holocaust*)

Testimony of Roma T. *Voices of the Holocaust.* Illinois Institute of Technology Archives. Interview Date September 24, 1946.

Published Memoirs

Berg, Mary. *Warsaw Ghetto: Diary of Mary Berg.* New York: L.B. Fischer Publishing Corp, 1945.

Bettelheim, Bruno. *The Informed Heart: Autonomy in a Mass Age.* New York: Avon Books, 1960.

Borowski, Tadeusz. *This way for the gas ladies and gentlemen.* trans. Barbara Vedder. New York: Penguin Books, 1959.

Buber-Neumann, Margarete. *Under Two Dictators,* trans. Edward Fitzgerald. London: Gollancz, 1949.

Elias, Ruth. *Triumph of Hope: From Theresienstadt and Auschwitz to Israel.* New York: John Wiley, 1998.

Fenelon, Fania. *Playing for Time*. New York: Atheneum Publishers, 1977.

Frome, Frieda. *Some Dare to Dream.* Iowa: Iowa University Press, 1988.

Heger, Heinz. *The Men with the Pink Triangle.* trans. David Fernbach. London: Gay Men's Press, 1980.

Heller, Fanya Gottesfeld. *Love In A World Of Sorrow: A Teenage Girl's Holocaust Memoirs.* Devora Publishing, 2005.

Isaacson, Judith Magyar. *Seed of Sarah: Memoirs of a Survivor.* Illinois: University of Illinois Press, 1990.

Klein, Cecile. *Sentenced To Live.* New York: Holocaust Library, 1988.

Kogon, Eugen. *Theory and Practice of Hell.* New York: Octagon Books, 1973.

Krause, Johanna. *Twice Persecuted: Surviving in Nazi Germany and Communist East Germany*. trans. Carolyn Gammon and Christiane Hemker. Waterloo: Wilfrid Laurier Press, 2007.

Lengyel, Olga. *Five Chimneys.* New York: Ziff Davis Publishers, 1947.

Lustig, Arnold. *Lovely Green Eyes.* New York: Arcade Publishing, 2002.

Perl, Gisella. *I was a Doctor in Auschwitz.* New York: Arno Press, 1979.

Schloss, Eva. *Eva's Story: A Survivor's Tale.* New York: W.H. Allen & Company, 1988.

Schulman, Faye. *A Partisan's Memoir. Women of the Holocaust.* Toronto: Second Story Press, 1995.

Secondary Sources:

Articles

Aolain, Ni. "Sex-based Violence and the Holocaust: A Reevaluation of Harms and Rights in International Law." *Yale Journal of Law and Feminism,* 12 (2002): 36-58.

Goldenberg, Myrna. "Lessons Learned from Gentle Heroism: Women's Holocaust Narratives." *The Annals of the American Academy of Political and Social Science,* (January 1996): 78-93.

Goldenberg, Myrna. "From a World Beyond: Women and the Holocaust," *Feminist Studies,* 22 (1996): 667-87.

Gottschall, "Explaining Wartime Rape." *The Journal of Sex Research,* Vol. 41, No. 2 (May 2004): 118-132.

Heineman, Elizabeth. "Sexuality and Nazism: The Doubly Unspeakable?" in *Journal of the History of Sexuality* 11, (2002): 22-66.

Henry, Nicola, Tony Ward & Matt Hirshberg. 'A multifactorial model of wartime rape,' *Aggression and Violent Behavior,* (2004): 535-562.

Hyman, Paula. "Gender and Jewish History," *Tikkun,* 3:1 (1988): 35-38.

Katz, Steven T. "Thoughts on the Intersection of Rape and Rassenchande during the Holocaust," *Modern Judaism,* Vol. 32, No. 3, (October 2012): 293-322.

Sinnreich, Helene. "And it was something we didn't talk about:" Rape of Jewish Women During the Holocaust." *Holocaust Studies: A Journal of Culture and History*, Vol. 14, No.2, (Autumn 2008): 1-22.

Timm, Anette. "Sex with a Purpose: Prostitution, Venereal Disease and Militarized Masculinity in the Third Reich." *Journal of the History of Sexuality,* 11, (2002): 223-255.

Turshen, Meredith. "The Political Economy of Violence against women during Armed Conflicts in Uganda." *Social Research,* 67, (2000): 803-824.

PhD Dissertations

Chambers, Beverley. "Sexual Villainy in the Holocaust." PhD
Dissertation, University of Ottawa, 2011.

Flaschka, Monika. "Rape, Race, and Gender in Nazi Occupied
Territories." PhD Dissertation, Kent University State, 2009.

Gertjejanssen, Wendy Jo. "Victims, Heroes, Survivors." PhD
Dissertation, University of Minnesota, 2004.

Houge, Anette. "Wartime Rape and Sexual Violence: A qualitative
analysis of perpetrators of sexual violence during the war in
Bosnia and Herzegovina." PhD Dissertation, University of
Oslo, 2008.

Books

Apenszlak, Jacob ed. *The Black Book of Polish Jewry: An Account
of Martyrdom of Polish Jewry.* New York: Roy Publishers,
1943.

Aroneanu, Eugene. *Inside the Concentration Camps: Eyewitness
Accounts of Life in Hitler's Death Camps,* trans. Thomas
Whissen. Westport: Praeger Publishers, 1996.

Baer, Elizabeth and Myrna Goldenberg ed. *Experience and
Expression: Women, The Nazis, and the Holocaust.* Detroit:
Wayne State University Press, 2003.

Barstow, Anne ed. *War's Dirty Secret: Rape, Prostitution and other Crimes Against Women,* Cleveland: Pilgrim Press, 2000.

Bartov, Omer. *Hitler's Army. Soldiers, Nazis and the War in the Third Reich.* New York: Oxford University Press, 1991.

Bartov, Omer. *The Eastern Front, 1941-45: German Troops and the Barbarisation of Warfare.* New York: Palgrave Macmillan, 2001.

Bartov, Omer. *Germany's War and the Holocaust: Disputed Holocaust.* New York: Cornell University Press, 2003.

Bauman, Zygmunt. *Modernity and the Holocaust.* New York: Cornell University Press, 2000.

Baumel, Judith. *Double Jeopardy: Gender and the Holocaust.* London: Vallentine Mitchell, 1998.

Bergen, Doris and Peter Hayes, ed. *Lessons and Legacies VIII: From Generation to Generation.* Northwestern University Press, 2008.

Braham, Randolph, ed. *Reflections of the Holocaust in Art and Literature.* New York: Columbia University Press, 1990.

Branche, Raphaelle and Fabrice Virgili ed. *Rape in Wartime.* New York: Palgrave Macmillan, 2012.

Bridenthal, Renate, Atina Grossman, and Marion Kaplan, ed. *When Biology became Destiny: Women in Weimar and Nazi Germany.* New York: Monthly Review Press, 1984.

Browning, Christopher. *Remembering Survival: Inside a Nazi-Slave Labor Camp.* New York: W.W. Norton & Company, Inc., 2010.

Brownmiller, Susan. *Against Our Will: Men, Women and Rape.* New York: Simon and Schuster, 1975.

Desbois, Patrick. *The Holocaust by Bullets.* New York: Palgrave Macmillan, 2008.

Ehrenburg, Ilya and Vasily Grossman, ed. *Complete Black Book of Russian Jewry.* New Jersey: Transaction Publishers, 2003.

Frankel, Benjamin, ed. *History in Dispute, Vol. 11: The Holocaust, 1933-1945.* Michigan: St. James Press, 1999.

Franklin, Ruth. *A Thousand Darknesses: Lies and Truth in Holocaust Fiction.* Oxford: University Press, 2010.

Friedman, Jonathon. *Speaking the Unspeakable: Essays on Sexuality, Gender and Holocaust Survivor Memory.* New York: University Press, 1966.

Fuchs, Esther, ed. *Women and the Holocaust: Narrative and Representation.* New York: University Press of America, 1999.

Gellately, Robert and Nathan Stoltzfus. *Social Outsiders in Nazi Germany*. Princeton and Oxford: Princeton University Press, 2001.

Goldenberg, Myrna and Amy Shapiro, ed. *Different Horrors, Same Hell: Gender and the Holocaust.* Seattle and London: University of Washington Press, 2013.

Goldstein, Joshua. *War and Gender: How Gender Shapes the War System and Vice Versa.* Massachusetts: Cambridge University Press, 2001.

Gottleib, Roger ed. *Thinking the Unthinkable.* New Jersey: Paulist Press, 1990.

Hagemann, Karen and Stefanie Schueler-Springorum, ed. *Home Front: The Military, War, and Gender in the Twentieth Century Germany.* Oxford: Berg, 2000.

Hedgepeth, Sonja, and Rochelle G. Saidel, ed. *Sexual Violence Against Women during the Holocaust.* Hanover and London: University Press of New England, 2010.

Heinemann, Marlene. *Gender and Destiny: Women Writers and the Holocaust.* New York: Greenwood Press, 1986.

Herzog, Dagmar, ed. *Sexuality and German Fascism,* New York and Oxford: Berghan Books, 2002.

Herzog, Dagmar. *Sex After Fascism: Memory and Morality in Twentieth Century Germany.* Princeton: Princeton University Press, 2005

Herzog, Dagmar and Peter Hayes, ed. *Lessons and Legacies VII: The Holocaust in International Perspectives.* Norwest University Press, 2006.

Herzog, Dagmar, ed. *Brutality and Desire: War and Sexuality in Europe's Twentieth Century.* New York: Palgrave Macmillan, 2009.

Hertzog, Esther ed. *Life, Death and Sacrifice: Women and Family in the Holocaust.* New York: Gefen, 2008.

Jewish Black Book Committee, *The Black Book: The Nazi Crime Against the Jewish People.* New York: Duel, Sloan and Pierce, 1946.

Karay, Felicia. *Death Comes in Yellow: Skarzysko-Kamienna Slave Labor Camp.* Amsterdam: Overseas Publishers Association, 1996.

Kelman, Herbert and Lee Hamilton, *Crimes of Obedience. Toward a Social Psychology of Authority and Responsibility.* New Haven and New York: Yale University Press, 1989.

Krall, Hanna. *Shielding the Flame: An Intimate Conversation with Dr. Marek Edelman, the Last Surviving Leader of the Warsaw*

Ghetto Uprising, trans. Joanna Stasinska. New York: Henry Holt & Company, 1986.

Kremer, Lillian, *Women's Holocaust Writing: Memory and Imagination.* Lincoln and London: University of Nebraska, 1999

Langer, Lawrence. *Preempting the Holocaust.* Yale University Press, 2000.

Langer, Lawrence. *Versions of Survival: The Holocaust and the Human Spirit.* Albany: State University of New York Press, 1982.

Lentin, Ronit. ed., *Gender and Catastrophe.* London & New York: Zed Books, 1997.

Lifton, Robert J. *The Nazi Doctors: Medical Killing and the Psychology of Genocide.* New York: Basic Books, 1986.

Lorentzen, Lois Ann and Jennifer Turpin, ed., *Women and War Reader.* New York: New York University Press, 1998.

MacKinnon, Catherine. *Are Women Human?: And Other International Dialogues.* Cambridge: Harvard University Press, 2006.

Miller, J. *One by One by One: Facing the Holocaust.* New York: Simon and Schuster, 1990.

Morrison, Jack. *Ravensbruck: Everyday life in a Women's Concentration Camp, 1939-45.* Princeton: Markus Wiener Publishers, 2000.

Moser, Caroline and Fiona C. Clark. *Victims, Perpetrators or Actors? Gender, Armed Conflict and Political Violence.* London and New York: Zed Books, 2001.

Mosse, George. *Nationalism and Sexuality: Respectability and Abnormal Sexuality in Modern Europe,* New York: Howard Fertig, 1985.

Niewyk, Donald. ed. *Fresh Wounds: Early Narratives of Holocaust Survival.* North Carolina: University of North Carolina Press, 1998.

Niewyk, Donald, ed. *The Holocaust.* Boston: Wadsworth Cengage Learning, 2011.

Ofer, Dalia, and Lenore J. Weitzman, ed. *Women in the Holocaust.* New Haven and London: Yale University Press, 1998.

Pike, David, ed. *Crimes Against Women.* New York: Nova Science Publishers, Inc., 2011.

Rhodes, Richard. *Masters of Death: The SS Einsatzgruppen and the Invention of the Holocaust.* New York: Random House, 2002.

Ringelheim, Joan and Esther Katz, ed., *Proceedings of the Conference on Women Surviving the Holocaust.* New York: Institute for Research in History, 1983.

Rittner, Carol and John K. Roth ed. *Different Voices: Women and the Holocaust.* New York: Paragon House, 1993.

Rittner, Carol and John K. Roth ed. *Rape: Weapon of War and Genocide.* Minnesota: Paragon House, 2012.

Ritvo, Roger and Dianne Plotki, *Sisters in Sorrow: Voices of Care in the Holocaust.* Texas: A & M University Press, 1998.

Saidel, Rochelle. *The Jewish Women of Ravensbruck Concentration Camp.* Wisconsin: The University of Wisconsin Press, 2004.

Sanday, Peggy. *Fraternity Gang Rape.* New York and London: New York University, 2007.

Seifert, Ruth ed. *Gender Dynamics and Post-Conflict Reconstruction.* New York: Peter Lang, 2009.

Shapiro, Moses, ed. *Lodz Ghetto: A History.* Bloomington: Indiana University Press, 2006.

Stiglmayer, Alexandra, ed. *Mass Rape: The War against Women in Bosnia-Herzegovina*, Lincoln and London: University of Nebraska Press, 1994.

Thornhill, Randy and Craig Palmer. *A Natural History of Rape.*
Massachusetts: The MIT Press, 2000.

Totten, Samuel, ed., *Plight and Fate of Women during and
following Genocide* (New Brunswick: Transaction Publishers,
2009.

Waxman, Zoe. *Writing the Holocaust: Identity, Testimony,
Representation.* Oxford: Oxford University Press, 2006.

ABOUT THE AUTHOR

Alana Fangrad was born in Mississauga, Ontario. She has an Honours Bachelor of Arts Degree and Masters Degree in History from the University of Western Ontario. She specializes in Modern European History and Women's Studies. In the future she intends to complete her PhD in History.

www.ingramcontent.com/pod-product-compliance
Lightning Source LLC
Chambersburg PA
CBHW050357290526
45786CB00003B/1020